Every Employee an Entrepreneur

How to Build a Highly Effective Organisation

Hiew Chok Sien

First published 2020 by:
Simplify People Resources
31, Jalan Budiman 21, Taman Mulia,
56000 Kuala Lumpur, Malaysia.

www.simplifypeople.com

ISBN 978-967-18562-0-8

Printed in Malaysia by Paperprinn On Demand

For Ba and Ma

Contents

Introduction: Why Would You Want Your Employees to be Entrepreneurs?...1

How this book is organised 5

Part 1: Success Factors...7

Chapter 1: The Value Mindset 9

Take Action 14

Chapter 2: Think Like a Boss...15

Building Leaders 17

Take Action 18

Chapter 3: The Learning Organisation - EMTC 21

The Explorer...22

The Matron...22

The Teenager..23

The Child..23

Take Action 25

Foundations of an Entrepreneurial Culture 27

Part 2: Assessment Tools 29

Chapter 4: Organisation Culture Type 31

Community..34

Freelance Agency...36

Research University 37

Young Start-up 38

Identifying Your Culture Type....................................40

What Will Work Best for You 44

Take Action 47

Chapter 5: Organisation Evolution 49

The Ad Hoc Stage 50

The Structured Stage 51

The Superstars Stage 53

The Win Together Stage 55

The Culture Evolution Analogy 56

Take Action 57

Part 3: Implementation 59

Chapter 6: Defining Your Purpose 61

The "Right" Purpose 61

Measure What's Important 62

Relate to Your Purpose 63

Praise Desired Behaviours 64

Remember to Reflect 64

Take Action 66

Chapter 7: Building Trust 67

Walk the Talk 67

Respect Every Individual 68

Practise Fairness 70

Keep Your Word 72

Trust Your Team 74

Be an Authority Figure 75

Take Action 77

Chapter 8: Communication - As A Leader..........................79

Listening..79

Psychological Safety 80

Purposeful Repetition....................................82

Say It 5 Times 83

Explain Both Good and Bad............................85

Take Action 87

Chapter 9: Communication - As an Organisation 89

Transparent Targets and Results 89

Regular Meetings 90

Town Halls 92

Surveys...93

Performance Appraisals 95

Team Building Activities 96

Terminations 97

Take Action 99

Culture Implementation Framework 100

Chapter 10: OTJM..103

Objective 103

Target Audience 104

Job to Be Done 105

Metrics...106

Case Study - Applying OTJM........................107

Take Action 109

Chapter 11: Breaking Rules 111

Endnotes 113

Further Reading 115

About the Author 117

Acknowledgements

I am grateful to K. C. See for inspiring me to write this book and to Gerry Robert for motivating me to get it done. I am thankful to my mentor and coach Jonathan Low, for his invaluable advice and insights.

I thank Allen Sam, Chew Meng Mei, Hiew Thien Choi, Kung Juk Len, Philip Lau Siu Chung, Yap Chee Seng, Pung Cherng Liang, and Lim Kee Wa for their support and feedback, without which the book would not be what it is today. I thoroughly enjoyed working with Edwin Chong of Morisan Studio on the book cover. My editor Jessie Raymond reaffirmed my belief that one must always strive to improve. I owe Tan Teck Seng on OTJM.

There are many leaders I have never met in person but have learned from and whose teachings I have been guided by. Some of these are listed in the section Further Reading. There are also many leaders and comrades whom I have worked with and learned from. I am grateful to both.

I thank my wife, Michelle Fu Yee Vun, for telling me - just do it.

Introduction: Why Would You Want Your Employees to be Entrepreneurs?

Picture this. You recruit this fresh graduate - hard worker, ambitious, street-smart, friendly, fits in well with your team. She is eager to learn and you are more than happy to mentor her. She delivers quality work. Very soon, you can let her operate independently. She makes the right decisions, and when in doubt, she seeks your guidance appropriately. In less than a year, she is already bringing in new clients for your company and growing your business. You reward her with a generous salary increment. You offer her equity. Then two years later, she tells you she is resigning. She partners with some friends and starts her own company. You lose some of your clients to her new company. All that you have taught her, and all the industry contacts you have introduced to her, have now equipped her to become a strong competitor. Your business takes a hit. Your protege has now become a threat. You wonder why you trained this successful entrepreneur, who would eventually betray you, and ultimately bring harm to your business which you have spent years building.

Let's imagine another scenario. You have started a successful business from scratch. You have unique skills and knowledge which give you an edge over your competitors. To grow your business, you need to recruit and build a team around you. You don't want superstars. You want people who can follow instructions meticulously, who are not calculative and don't mind working long hours, who understand you and don't complain, who get the job done on time and with quality and who don't play politics or cause trouble. You train your employees just enough to enable them to do their respective jobs efficiently. You protect your trade secrets. You fire people who don't fit in, those who overestimate themselves and make unreasonable demands, and those who don't believe in your vision. You don't spoon-feed them. You want them to buck up or get out. You are wary of overly ambitious employees who do not have the best interests of the company in mind. As you grow your staff, you maintain strong control of your people, your knowledge, your trade secrets and your competitive edge. You are not going to have a situation of the disciple killing the master. You are not going to train someone who will eventually stab you in the back.

That's how the stereotypical Chinese kung-fu master thinks.

Let's look at some specific situations.

An urgent issue comes up. A long-time VIP customer threatens to go public on an incident in which your sales rep has allegedly deceived him. Despite having established a comprehensive set of standard operating procedures (SOP's) for your staff, no rule explicitly addresses this situation. No one on your team is sure what to do. They can do their individual jobs competently, but they don't have the full picture and they can't make strategic decisions which affect multiple departments. You are overseas and they are not even sure whether they should call you. They eventually do, after some delay. By then, the damage is already done. You wish you had someone who could think like you and act quickly like you, and make the right decisions.

Let's do another.

It has been a long day. You have had meeting after meeting with your teams. They bring you problems but no solutions, not even options. They ask you for approval for small things, which make you question their competence. You cannot understand why they do not have the right mindset and do not know how to prioritise. It's common sense! You feel surrounded by idiots. You are doing all the work. You become the bottleneck. Things don't move unless you push. Your staff doesn't seem to care if the company is doing well. They just sit and wait for your directions. They don't understand how you worry about having enough money in the bank account to pay their salaries every month.

If you want a high-performance team, if you want to have a company which works effectively, you must make every employee think like an entrepreneur. Entrepreneurs are a special breed. Most people go through life following a prescribed path. We go through school, we find a job, we climb to higher and higher positions, then we retire and comfortably enjoy our final years. Entrepreneurs are mad people who go off the beaten path into the unknown. These people are curious and courageous. They are driven and determined. They are pragmatic and open-minded. They are "abnormal", but they are probably what the world needs; people who solve problems and create value. In a fast-changing world, organisations need to adapt and change with the times.

To have a high-performance team, you must nurture your employees, and you must not hold back. If you want them to be able to stand in for you, you need to train them well enough to run the business as competently as you can, or even better. If you want them to be able to think like you, you must have clear and consistent communication. You must inspire them to share the same vision as you, so that they will become more creative in solving problems and helping the organisation achieve its goal. Give them clear principles to guide their decision-making.

And what about the backstabbers? If your protege is able to steal your customers, you probably deserve it. It means she is serving them better than you are. Business is business. Humankind makes progress. If you do not continuously improve, you will be left behind, and that is right. No one owes any company any loyalty. It is unreasonable to expect such. We owe loyalty to our principles and ideals, and to our friends and family, but never to the concept of a company. It is just a paper entity born out of the desire of investors to make more money, and it employs people. An employment is a mutually beneficial business relationship. An employee gives your company his time, his skills and his experience, helping your company make more money than what you pay him. Your company pays him a stable salary, and he gains knowledge, maybe reputation, and hopefully, friendship and community too. An employment arrangement thrives only when both parties continue to receive what they want, which can change over time. If the expectations of an employee diverge from that of the company, why expect him to stay? It is neither reasonable nor beneficial to either party.

We want our employees and ex-employees to do well. We want a society with kind and capable people, who create value for everyone and make the world a better place. Ultimately, we pursue the greater good. Life is not a narrow, zero-sum game. If your employee leaves you and becomes more successful, it should be celebrated. Worrying about employees leaving because you have trained them well is a silly thing to do if you haven't even trained and coached them well enough for your day-to-day operations. If your business is running smoothly and you have a team of strong and ambitious employees, you must continue to challenge them and challenge yourself to create even more value for yourself, for them, and for society.

How this book is organised

The content of this book is organised into three sections.

1. Success Factors
2. Assessment Tools
3. Implementation

The Success Factors section describes the key elements of a high-performance organisation. It explains important mindsets to instil in your organisation. The Assessment Tools section provides perspectives to analyse and understand your organisation, and to identify the gaps you want to close. The Implementation section lists practices and processes you can apply in how you carry yourself, build a strong team around you, and instil an entrepreneurial culture in your organisation.

The Success Factors are your destination. The Assessment Tools will tell you where you are now. The Implementation will guide you to go from here to there.

Part 1: Success Factors

Chapter 1: The Value Mindset

Fan Deng said, "If you want to become an entrepreneur because you want to make more money, stop. It is the wrong place to start, and you may not last long." If your focus is on self-enrichment and you are not obsessed with bringing value to your target customers, you may not survive the difficult journey of launching and sustaining a new business. A business will only survive if it brings value to the table. It doesn't necessarily have to be unique or new, but the product or service it delivers must be something that the customers believe in and will continue to buy.

We must always challenge ourselves on what value we bring every day. It forces us to be creative, to find problems to solve, and ultimately, to increase the value that we bring. As the employer, one straightforward method we often use is, we compare the cost of an employee against the revenue he generates for the company. This method is rather blunt and not ideal, but it's not unfair. The value of an employee is not measured only in monetary terms. The value of a company or an organisation may not necessarily be measured in monetary terms alone. Understanding the value is important. Agreeing on the value we want to bring is important. That is the mission of your organisation.

You want your employee to understand the value your organisation is trying to bring to the world. It drives day-to-day decision-making. It sets training priorities. Understanding it drives the desired behaviour in your teams.

IKEA's value proposition is to offer well-designed and practical furniture at low prices so that many people can afford them.

When you visit an IKEA store and browse its products, you will find that they reflect this guiding principle. Many products do not use high quality wood and that is in line with keeping their products affordable. You assemble the furniture yourself so there is no need for IKEA to employ people to do this. This keeps prices low too. Walking through an IKEA showroom is like exploring a treasure chest. You often come across clever ideas on saving space. You discover clever utensils you never realised you needed. All this is driven by IKEA's promise of value.

You must begin to instil the value mindset the day you interview a candidate. Ask him what value he wants to get from the organisation. The answer may be money, or learning opportunities, or future prospects, or fulfilling work. You want your organisation to be able to provide what the candidate wants. Then, ask what he thinks he can contribute to the organisation. How will he help increase the value the organisation brings to its customers? Start an employment relationship on a business partner footing. Both parties must bring value to the deal, and must never take the other party for granted.

Encourage employees to increase their value. What they learn is theirs to keep, even if they leave. They learn not only from formal training, but also from observing others, asking questions, seeking guidance and taking initiative to improve customer experience and existing processes. In some organisations, employees expect annual salary increments and annual bonuses. This is often a point of disagreement between company and staff. On one hand, the company thinks if you are not helping the company earn more money than the previous year, why should I pay you more? That is fair, and that is also why the company must help its employees improve and grow. When an employee is bringing more value to the company (and value is not only reflected in sales) the company must acknowledge and reward this. An employee with a value mindset understands that salary and bonus simply reflect the value he brings to the team, and knows that the more he contributes and achieves, the more he will receive. People with the value mindset are not self-entitled.

It is important to constantly challenge the norm. Humans are beings of habits. We get so used to this weekly meeting and that daily report, that we lose sight of whether they are even useful anymore. If something no longer brings value, simplify it, or cut it out completely. Spend your time and energy doing something more useful. Ask your employees to have the courage to challenge convention and organisational habits.

The first London Underground map, published in 1908, was very different from what we see today. It had Underground lines drawn directly on top of an accurate street map of London. The map was a pain to use. The twisting and overlapping Underground lines, although geographically correct, were difficult to read. Station names were small and had to be written at odd angles in order to fit them all in. Stations further from the city centre were not shown, because to show them, the whole map would have to be zoomed out, making everything too small to read. In 1931, Harry Beck created a map that looked like what we have today. At the time, it was a ground-breaking map which challenged many conventions. Why place the Underground map on a real map? Why show accurate relative distances between stations? An Underground passenger doesn't need to know the exact shape of an Underground line. She only needs to know it connects stations A and B. A straight line works just fine. Readability is of higher value than geographical accuracy. Beck discarded what was of little value and focused on what brought value.

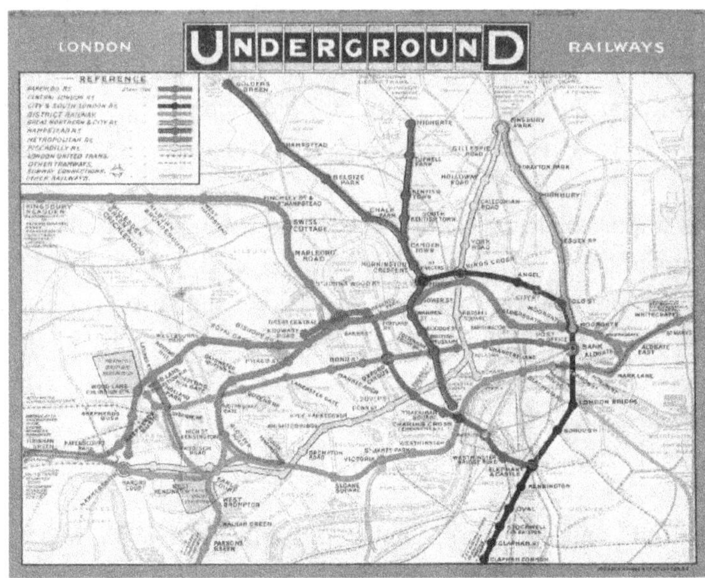

The original London Underground map, 1908.
© TfL from the London Transport Museum collection

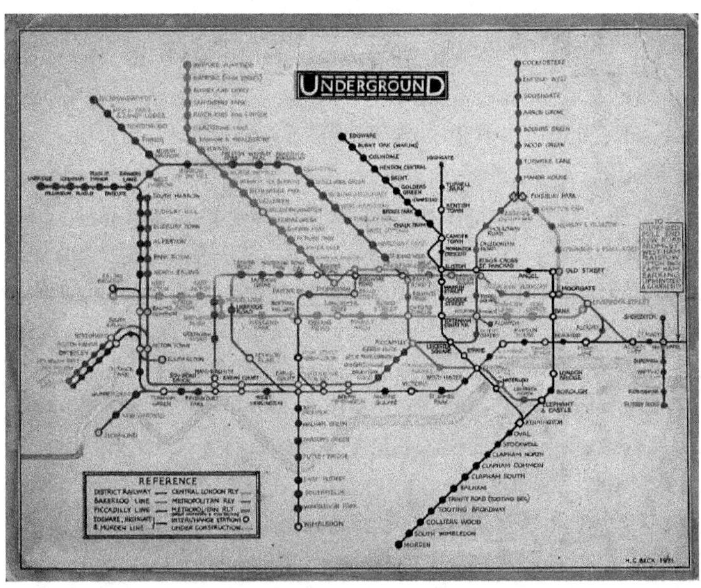

The London Underground map by Harry Beck, 1931.
© TfL from the London Transport Museum collection

When we manage teams, it is easy to direct team members to generate this weekly report or that daily analysis. We just give the order and let other people worry about getting the work done. If your team forgets to do the report once, and you don't realise it until the next time the report is due, then you don't really need it and you should scrap it or simplify it.

Continuing to do something which no longer brings value is wasteful. In this age of ubiquitous smartphones, you should not be aggressively deploying public payphones. Yet many don't realise we continue to do low-value tasks because of habit, and because we don't challenge the value.

Take Action

On a blank piece of paper, write down today's date and your answers to these questions. Take time to think about them before writing. In future, whenever you feel uncertain, come back to this piece of paper to remind yourself of the values of your organisation.

1. What business is my organisation in?
2. Who am I helping? What problem am I solving?
3. What is it about how I conduct my business that makes my customers value me?
4. If my organisation disappears tomorrow, will it be a loss to the world? Who would miss us?
5. How am I measuring my value or the value of my organisation?
6. What am I doing now which is of little to no value and should be discarded or changed?
7. If I have found where my true value lies, what will I do to enhance that?

Chapter 2: Think Like a Boss

When business owners and managers share challenges that they face, one common challenge is competency level of their employees. A common consolation you have probably heard is, "If they were smart, they would be sitting in your position!" Does this mean you have to accept and live with semi-competent employees? Definitely not! You want a boss mindset in your employees, so that the company can still run without you being involved in many operational details, giving you space to do other things. You want your people to do more and more of what you can do, i.e. the most valuable tasks, so that you can spend time to look for more opportunities to create new value.

Why do employees not think like bosses? Typically, employees are trading their lives for salaries. Work is just something they grudgingly do because they need to make a living. They only care about getting paid at the end of the month. They live for weekends, when they don't have to work. On Wednesdays, they celebrate hump day, because half the work week is over. They have a narrow focus. They just want to get their tasks done and they don't even want to do them too efficiently, so that they don't get "rewarded" with more tasks! They have paid their (hopefully productive) 40 hours per week to the company and they are not going to give anything more than what is in the employment agreement.

With this mentality, it is no surprise that many companies stagnate and become inefficient. Employees don't put in their creativity. Leaders struggle to motivate their people. Sometimes neither carrots nor sticks work. They can even make things worse.

You want your people to think like bosses, because you want them to have these two things:

1. Ownership
2. Strategic Thinking

Having ownership means truly caring about your work and wanting to get it done well. It is about understanding how your work fits in to the organisation's goals and purpose, and why it is important. Ownership means caring about how your work affects your immediate teammates, your fellow colleagues from other departments and the company as a whole. Ownership means always striving to do right by your customers. Employees with strong ownership always improve, because they take pride in their work. They are dependable.

Strategic thinking is crucial to making the right decisions. The last thing you want is to be interrupted every 30 minutes for one decision after another because your teams are not confident enough to make the call. You want your teams to have the confidence to make decisions. Making decisions is not only about daring to do so without consulting you. It is also important that they make the *right* decisions. Deciding whether they need to consult you is also a decision in itself.

By having strategic thinking, your teams will have the full picture and a strong understanding of the implications of the decisions. They don't need you to tell them what to do all the time. They will only catch you for critical decisions. Otherwise, they just update you on what's been done, what the risks are, the reasoning behind the decision and the current progress.

Building Leaders

An important element of growing a business is having teams who think ahead of you. As a team or an organisation grows, it becomes impossible for you to do everything yourself. If you are the only person worrying about everything, while others sit and wait for your instructions, you will find yourself drained. You want employees who can start taking over certain areas from you, and think ahead of you in those areas. As you coach your immediate reports, you will find that you are creating a close-knit team which is more than the sum of its parts. New ideas are often born from discussions and debates. So are solutions to complex problems.

When you have an organisation where all the members think like bosses, it becomes much easier for you to find people you can promote and entrust important tasks / jobs / departments to.

Take Action

On a blank piece of paper, draw the following table. Put the people in your organisation into the appropriate boxes. If you have a large organisation, work with the leaders and managers first, or work based on departments or teams. Each person / team must appear twice, once in the Ownership column, and once in the Strategic Thinking column.

Behaviour	Ownership	Strategic Thinking
Consistently Demonstrating		
Occasionally Demonstrating		
Showing Potential		
Low Potential		

You will find three types of gaps:

1. If people are not consistently demonstrating both behaviours, this needs to be improved.
2. If the same person / team has higher Ownership than Strategic Thinking, this is a blind doer situation, where they work hard, but not necessarily smart enough.
3. If the same person / team has higher Strategic Thinking than Ownership, this is the talker situation, where they

have the capability, but not the motivation or commitment to get the work done.

Low Potential members of the organisation do not necessarily need to be removed. It may be a personal life choice of some people to play only certain roles in an organisation. Respect that. For example, a person may be content staying a call centre agent for the rest of his career, without ever wanting to become a team leader or a manager. He doesn't want to climb the corporate ladder. He only wants a stable income to sustain his standard of living. He spends his personal time enjoying art and making art.

Some Low Potential cases may be a matter of capability. If there are roles in the organisation which fit these members, they can still fill such roles well.

Chapter 3: The Learning Organisation - EMTC

Technology is accelerating how the world changes. In 2017, the average age of a Fortune 500 company was under 20 years, compared to the 1950s, when the average age was about 60 years. Many industries and businesses are being made obsolete by new technology and new business models. Movie rental shops have disappeared because watching movies online is cheap and convenient. Businesses innovate and improve, and those which remain stagnant risk being left behind by the market. Even phone scammers have been using IVR systems (Interactive Voice Response) to scale up their operations, to improve efficiency and to sound more convincing to their would-be victims. An organisation that is not learning, adapting, and when necessary, pivoting its business, risks dying a slow (and sometimes not so slow) death. Nokia was a top mobile phone maker in the world, but failed to adapt to the emergence of the smartphone. Their CEO, Stephen Elop famously said, "We didn't do anything wrong, but somehow, we lost."

During the 2020 COVID-19 pandemic when governments around the world imposed lockdowns, retail businesses were severely impacted. Some went bust, but some learned and adapted. Some enterprising grocers - and these were just small local businesses - set up shop on Facebook and sold pre-set grocery packages. There were only a few different packages to pick from, and what you picked mostly depended on how big your family was and how long you needed the food to last. A package included meats, vegetables, eggs, seasonings, sauces - all the items you typically see in a grocery shopping cart. During the lockdown when people were heavily restricted from grocery shopping, and were also afraid of going to public places, such a service became highly valued. These small-scale grocers did good business, because they learned and adapted quickly. They also implemented the pre-set package approach to make their fulfilment efficient and streamlined. When I describe it this way, you may see this as some slick internet start-up with venture capitalist funding, but this is really just local mom and pop stores learning to sell on Facebook.

What does it mean to become a learning organisation? There are four roles you need to play.

The Explorer

Keep looking for new ideas, improvements and opportunities. The Explorer is adventurous and curious. He hungers for knowledge. He loves the unknown. He is a pioneer. He is the spearhead. He dives into uncharted waters and is keen to learn a completely new field. He steps out of his comfort zone.

The Matron

The Matron is the passive counter-persona to the Explorer's active persona. She is quiet, thoughtful, observant and sensitive. She is wise and cunning. She has a network of little birds feeding her data, some of which may seem inconsequential, but she is able to discern what is important. She pieces things together to understand how the world is changing and why.

The Teenager

The Teenager is reckless and not afraid of getting hurt. Just Do It. You Only Live Once. By doing, and by failing, he learns. By failing quickly and early, he gains valuable experience faster than others who are conservative. The Teenager is passionate and follows his heart. He experiments. He acts.

The Child

We are all burdened and bound by our upbringing and personal experiences. Often, we don't recognise, or we deny, the limiting beliefs we carry with us through life. The older we get, the more confident we become of our worldviews. "That's how things are." "People are like that." "That's the reality you have to accept." The Child has no such inhibitions. She will ask why and then, she will ask why not. She has no preconceived notions; she's a blank slate. She is completely open-minded. Adults easily dismiss new ideas that don't align with their beliefs. The Child takes every idea seriously. Tweak it a little and a stupid idea may become a eureka moment. The Child challenges convention. The Child gives you fresh eyes on something you think you know like the back of your hand.

Continuously learning and training is a necessity when technology changes so fast. By the time a programmer completes his four-year university course, there will probably be a new programming language or tool that he needs to learn from scratch. If you are not watching how your competitors are improving, you will be left behind. In fact, you want to learn and improve faster than them, to stay ahead in the game.

C. C. Puan, founder and CEO of Green Packet, a listed company on the Kuala Lumpur Stock Exchange, is an avid reader. I once asked him how he managed it despite his busy schedule. He told me simply, "I just hack it!" He found time to listen to audiobooks when exercising. He both listened to audiobooks and read the physical books to better absorb the content. He applied what he learned to his businesses. Never stop learning, never stagnate.

A learning organisation is a nimble organisation. Being nimble means being able to react quickly to situations. When an organisation is open-minded and alert, it does not resist change. It is able to let go of established practices which are no longer useful. It is ready to embrace change, and can therefore adapt.

One industry greatly affected by the 2020 COVID-19 pandemic was the training industry. When face-to-face meetings were disallowed, many training seminars had to be postponed or cancelled. Some trainers quickly adapted by converting their content to become teachable via video conferencing tools like Zoom, Skype and Microsoft Teams. Some trainers converted their courses to recordings to be uploaded to online learning platforms like Udemy and Coursera. Trainers who failed to adapt saw their business grind to a halt. They also lost out on opportunities to reach out to new markets.

Sources of learning are not limited to new technology and new business trends. Your customers are an important source of learning. So are your employees. Learning from customers includes having salespersons speaking to them to understand their pain points, using instant messaging to collect feedback after services are performed, and tweaking a product and monitoring how well it sells. Learning from employees includes visiting the factory floor to ask about problems they face, measuring how policy changes affect productivity and having open forums to encourage suggestions and questions.

Learning is not limited to just the training courses your HR team schedules for your staff. Play all four roles to maximise learning in the organisation.

Take Action

1. On a blank piece of paper, draw the table below. Examine your own learning behaviours. Which of the four roles do you currently play? Write down the things you do which show that you are currently playing one or more of the learning roles.

Explorer	**Matron**
Teenager	**Child**

The EMTC Diagram

2. On a new sheet, using the same table, list members in your organisation (eithers persons or teams) who play one or more of the learning roles. Some members may play more than one role. If you find some members not playing any learning role, that may be an opportunity for improvement. If you find nobody plays a certain learning role, that is a gap your organisation needs to fill.

3. On a new sheet, using the same table, list activities in your organisation which reflect one or more of the learning roles being played. Are these effective? Do they need to be improved? What are activities that should be added to address these gaps?

Foundations of an Entrepreneurial Culture

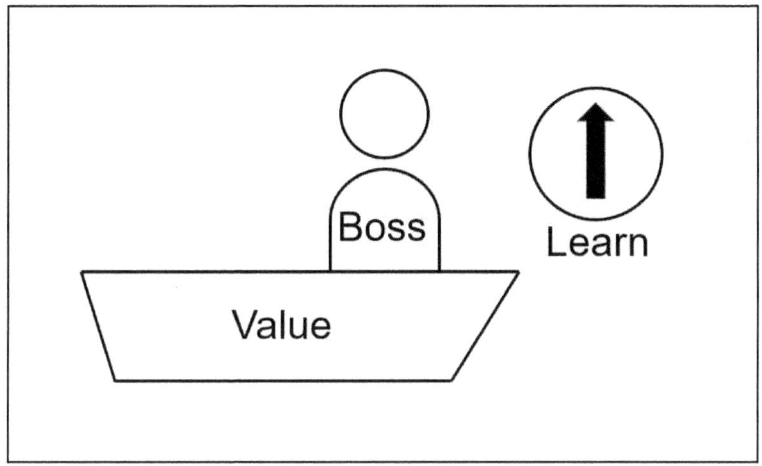

Foundations of an Entrepreneurial Culture

The success factors are summarised in the diagram above. The value mindset is the hull of the ship. If an organisation does not create or deliver value, it will not stay afloat. Thinking like a boss is the captain. The captain must always have a strategic view in order to run the ship, and certainly the captain takes ownership and has accountability. Without a boss mindset, an organisation cannot operate effectively. The learning culture is the compass. The compass guides the ship out of difficulties. It helps to chart a course and keeps the ship moving forward. An organisation which does not learn and adapt will stagnate and eventually lose its value.

Part 2: Assessment Tools

Chapter 4: Organisation Culture Type

How do you describe the culture at your organisation? Do you have a systematic way of describing and comparing your organisation's culture against other organisations'? Whether you lead a small team, or manage a large company, as long as you bring people to work together on a daily basis, you will have a culture. An organisation's culture can be distilled down to two things:

1. Collective mindset
2. Expected behaviours

An organisation will share certain values and will think alike on many principles. It is only natural. New members will be influenced by the tribe and become more like them. Those who do not fit in will eventually leave. Over time, through day-to-day interactions, the group settles down to some common ways of thinking; an equilibrium, if you will. This is why sometimes when we ask a new acquaintance where he works, and he tells us his company name, in our mind we raise an eye-brow and think, "oh he is that kind of person". Some companies have cultures which are well known even outside the industry. Southwest Airlines has a culture that stands out. People think of them as happy, friendly and fun, as opposed to grumpy and unhelpful, as is typical in the airline industry.

The culture of your organisation determines the expected behaviour people have. It decides what the norm is. Given a certain situation or crisis, there is a "right" way that people are expected to behave. It is not just about procedures and rules. It is the values of the people which tell them what feels right to do. When something outside of the ordinary happens, and it is not described in the Standard Operating Procedures, an employee will still know what to do, because she understands the values of the company. She knows what feels right to do. She is simply living the values of the company. It is a second nature born out of the company culture.

One good example is a game community manager, CK, whom I have worked with. He managed an old online game which was near end of life but still had a small community of loyal players. Some of them still regularly spent on the game, which allowed us to continue to operate the game profitably. Once, one of the loyal players contacted him and requested for a deep discount on some in-game items. The player wanted to buy in bulk, and wanted to try his luck in getting a discount. CK made the decision there and then, securing the sale and making a customer very happy. We did not have specific rules for this situation. In fact, normally we did not allow discounts because it would devalue our in-game currencies. However, CK understood that in the case of this particular old game, it was maintained only because of this small group of spending players. Managing the game was basically servicing this small group of players. We were not going to revive or expand this old game anymore. CK was clear on what was expected and acted appropriately, without needing to consult his manager or agonise over procedures.

Culture is important to an organisation because it is equivalent to a person's personality, attitude and mindset. Just as these determine a person's success in a career path he has chosen, a company's culture determines whether it survives and how far it will grow. There is no "correct" culture to adopt for your organisation. You need to first understand your current organisation culture, understand what works and what doesn't for your industry, your business environment and the current state of your organisation, and finally, you have to choose what will work best for you. That may not even be the end. As the business environment changes and as your organisation grows and evolves, you need to revisit and recalibrate. You must remain a learning organisation!

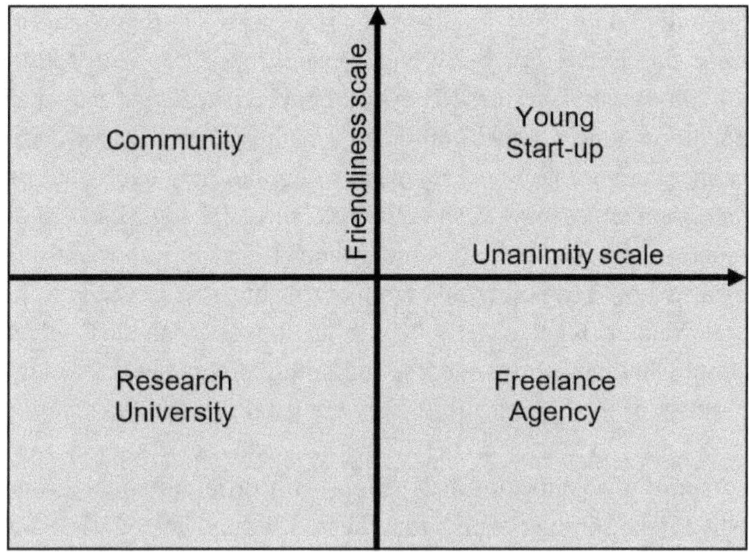

Organisation culture can be categorised into four types using two scales - Friendliness and Unanimity. Friendliness is a measure of how strong personal relationships are in the organisation. In a high-Friendliness organisation, the cleaner is on a first name basis with the CEO. Employees are personal friends outside of work, meeting up for sports, for dinners and even going on holidays together. Workers take a genuine interest in and care for one another. Personal relationships are important. It is a lot about who you know, not just what you know. In a low-Friendliness organisation, relationships are mostly professional. Not that people are hostile, just that colleagues are colleagues and not friends. It is understood that colleagues don't often mix outside of work and team-building activities. People respect and take care of one another at the workplace, but there is no expectation of getting personal. Everyone is happy operating in a professional context. It's just business.

Unanimity is a measure of how closely the goals and values of the individuals in an organisation are aligned. Do they want the same thing? Do they behave in the same way? Do they follow the same unspoken rules? They need not be friends and they may not know one another's children's names, but when a crisis happens, they know exactly what to do and they can count on one another to play their respective roles. A high-Unanimity organisation has a clear value system (what is important and what is not) and commonly agreed priorities (what needs to be done and in what order). People are honest with themselves about what constitutes success and failure. People believe in the purpose of the organisation. They are single-minded in wanting to get the job done, and they expect the same of others. A low-Unanimity organisation has people with different agendas and objectives, some of which may be conflicting. There are many different ways of doing things, and often, there is no single right way.

Let's examine the four culture types based on different levels of Friendliness and Unanimity.

Community

High Friendliness, Low Unanimity

The Community type organisation is like a big family. Many large, established and traditional companies have this culture type. Employees have known one another for many years. Often, things get done through relationships. Need help with an urgent issue? Let's talk to the department head. She is close with the marketing manager and the customer service team leader and may be able to get them to assign some resources to help out. Don't waste time writing long emails or waiting for the next inter-departmental meeting. Just go talk to people.

Community type companies often have happier employees and good retention. There is strong unity, as in people take care of one another. This is different from Unanimity. People may have different opinions and ways of working (low Unanimity), but can still be equally loyal to their team. The Community type organisation is supportive and helpful. It is tolerant. It is easier to build trust in a Community type organisation.

One common problem of Community type organisations is cliques. Because of how personal relationships play an important role, if you are not part of a clique, you may find it difficult getting things done. Sometimes, you are among the in group, and sometimes you are not. You can speed things up when you are among the in group, but you may get resistance when you are not. The way a Community operates can lead to biased decision-making, inefficiencies, processes being bypassed and poor meritocracy. There can be inconsistencies and double standards. In extreme cases, you see favouritism, nepotism and turf wars. A Community culture can lead to complacency, when a company behaves more like a family than a business. All the above remind us of one word - politics. Indeed, Community type organisations can end up being political.

Freelance Agency

Low Friendliness, High Unanimity

Let's look at the other extreme. The Freelance Agency type is all business and no niceties. You are here to get the job done and not to socialise. Imagine an agency which works with a loose group of freelance artists. When a new job comes in, it tries to find whoever is available, has the right skills and preferred style, and charges a fee within the client's budget. Naturally, this model is mercenary in nature. The freelancers do not necessarily compete ruthlessly undercutting one another. Everyone knows the rules of the game and plays by them.

In a Freelance Agency type culture, people operate in a transactional, almost cold, way. It is expected and there are no hard feelings. People are brutally efficient. People believe in swim or sink. If you are not contributing, why are you still here? There is high meritocracy. Good work is rewarded, and good work means results, not just effort. Don't waste time. We know what we are here for, let's be focused on getting the job done. We are professionals.

Naturally, it can be stressful working in a Freelance Agency type culture. It is everyone for himself / herself and dog-eat-dog. Employees can be highly competitive and ruthless. Loyalty is low. When an employee finds a better offer elsewhere, there is little reason to stay. The work atmosphere is intense, and the work environment can be unforgiving. Sometimes, intense competition leads to unscrupulous behaviour.

One company I have come across is an extreme example of a Freelance Agency type culture. They employ people around the world, and their staff all work from home. This practice started well before the 2020 COVID-19 pandemic. Employees all work on a contract basis, and contracts can be terminated at short notice if performance doesn't meet expectations. The company uses video cameras and keyboard keystroke monitors to detect whether employees are working at their computers during their work hours. Effective work is measured and tracked this way. Employees are paid only for effective work done. Results are reviewed every week.

This sounds like a horrible organisation to work for. You are being watched all the time. You don't even feel comfortable taking a short break. Every week, you are under pressure to produce results, and you wonder whether the next bad review will mean losing your job. Yet, this model works! For those who can adapt to the culture, they find that it helps bring out the best in them. They are performing and achieving. They are also paid well. They have flexible hours. The constant monitoring is considered fair play.

Research University

Low Friendliness, Low Unanimity

A low Friendliness and low Unanimity workplace may seem like a terrible idea. It is important to note that none of the four culture types are inherently good or bad. It is a matter of what best suits the organisation, the business environment / industry, and the people. A research university is a good example of how low Friendliness and low Unanimity work perfectly. Research professors work on diverse projects, leading different teams. They focus on their respective studies and don't need to mingle or depend on one another. They operate in different ways. They are highly specialised in their respective fields.

People in a Research University type culture have much freedom. They work independently. They are responsible for their own success. They get to apply their creativity to solve their vastly different problems. They offer highly customised solutions and experiences to their respective customers and stakeholders, who have different needs and expectations.

When you work in a Research University type culture organisation, sometimes, you barely feel like you belong to an organisation. You are doing your own thing. The organisation is fragmented. There is not much of a support system or people network you can fall back on. People work behind closed doors. Often, individual agendas and the organisation's agenda are different. It is hard to cooperate or create synergy.

Even large, established companies may have a Research University type culture. Let's imagine a global pharmaceutical company. If its modus operandi is many independent teams and subsidiaries developing and marketing different products, serving different customers and market segments, then it has a Research University type culture.

Young Start-up

High Friendliness, High Unanimity

A Young Start-up type organisation sounds like an ideal workplace, and it is hard to imagine what the drawbacks could possibly be. A typical start-up is a small group of enthusiastic people who keenly believe in a new business idea or technology and are determined to turn it into a successful and sustainable business. They are highly motivated and committed. They work hard. They encourage and take care of one another. They are willing to make sacrifices because of their strong conviction. They are a close-knit tribe. They are dreamers. They are passionate about their work and because of that, they are focused and productive. Typically, the leaders of such organisations are visionary, charismatic and inspiring.

So what can be wrong? For one thing, it is often not easy to sustain a Young Start-up culture. As an organisation grows, you get more and more people with different mindsets, goals and attitudes. Not everyone wants to work in a Young Start-up type culture. This type of culture can consume a person's life. Being passionate about your calling, and being a workaholic, are sometimes not easy to tell apart. Even the mindsets and attitudes of the founding members of a start-up can change over time. A Young Start-up type working environment is an intense one. It is highly rewarding but also highly demanding. It is not easy to be unwaveringly positive and gung-ho all the time. We are only human. It is important not to fake a Young Start-up culture for your organisation. It only becomes insincere and your efforts will be ineffective.

A Young Start-up type organisation can sometimes be blindsided. When everyone thinks and behaves the same way, you lose diversity. You lose the perspectives of people who think differently. A group of people with a strong Young Start-up culture may seem exclusive to people not like them. Aloof, even. Sometimes, they are perceived as detached from reality. If an organisation splits into one Young Start-up group and one Others group, it is a sign of danger. There may be misalignment in their objectives and communication breakdown.

Community
  Belonging
  Support
  Cliques
  Inefficient
	Young Start-up
	  Passion
	  Commitment
	  Unsustainable
	  Workaholics

Research University
  Freedom
  Diverse / customised
    solutions
  Low alignment
  Low cooperation
	Freelance Agency
	  Effective
	  Practical
	  Meritocracy
	  Transactional
	  Unforgiving

The vertical axis is labelled **Friendliness** and the horizontal axis is labelled **Unanimity**.

Selecting a culture to strive for is based on understanding your people and your business environment. What will work best for you? Where do you currently stand? Recognising where you are and where you want to be will give you an idea on what needs to be done and what needs to change.

Identifying Your Culture Type

By understanding the four culture types, you may already clearly see which type your organisation has. If it is not yet clear, the methods described below will help. They will also help to verify your judgement if you think you already know where your organisation stands.

You may find that different groups within your organisation have different cultures. This can be due to different leadership styles of their leaders or dominant influencers. It is not necessarily a bad thing. In some cases, it is desirable. E.g. the head office of an insurance company may have a Community type culture, while its network of insurance agents has a Freelance Agency culture. Take this into account when identifying your culture type, and when determining which will work best for you.

These questions will help you determine the culture type(s) of your organisation.

Community:
1. Are you friends with your colleagues? Do you meet outside of work?
2. Do people proactively offer help when a colleague is in difficulty?
3. Can you count on colleagues for a favour when you need something urgently, sometimes temporarily bypassing procedures?
4. Do you notice some clusters of close friends at the office?
5. Do you feel awkward about giving negative feedback to a peer or a subordinate?
6. Are some people perceived as the boss' favourite?
7. Do teams operate on a rule-by-consensus basis? Everyone's input is sought, and the team makes a decision that is not offensive to anyone.
8. Are leaders forgiving about unmet targets, as long as team spirit and unity are upheld?

Freelance Agency:
1. Is there a strong focus on reporting and reviewing results?
2. Are rewards and compensation directly linked to individual performance?

3. People do not have preferences to work with any particular colleagues, because they trust in the professionalism and competency of anyone assigned to work with them?
4. Are low performers quickly given feedback and dismissed if they do not show improvement?
5. Colleagues don't often chat about personal or family life?
6. People eat lunch at their cubicles and rarely socialise?
7. Is ruthless competition accepted as practical and matter-of-fact?
8. People with different personalities are able to collaborate well because when it comes to work, they share the same values and expectations?

Research University:
1. Are teams able to operate mostly independently in a decentralised manner, while remaining effective?
2. Different departments serve different customers / regions / industries with little overlap?
3. Small teams have freedom to make decisions about serving their stakeholders, and do not need to seek HQ approval?
4. Some teams have no idea what some other teams are doing?
5. Are you comfortable with working on your own tasks without needing any support from other teams? In fact, you do not expect others to be able to help you much?
6. People sitting near one another don't know their names and rarely speak?
7. Teams have very different work styles, but this does not cause conflict at work?
8. Different teams define success and priorities differently?

Young Start-up:
1. Do many employees come to work early, stay late, and work evenings or weekends without being asked to?
2. Do team members feel comfortable giving negative feedback directly without worrying about hurting one another's feelings?
3. Do leaders regularly celebrate successes or milestones with their teams? E.g. lunch / dinner celebrations, birthday celebrations.
4. Do you see yourselves as a tribe?
5. Do you see personal sacrifices as necessary to achieve a greater good?
6. Do you always feel motivated by a clear goal that is shared with everyone on the team?
7. Friends at work are among your closest circles of friends?
8. People genuinely enjoy the work they do together, and there is a strong spirit which helps them overcome hardships together?

If you have many YES' in a particular culture type, then your organisation has that type. In addition to asking yourself these questions, you can also pose these and similar questions to members of your organisation. E.g. using surveys. These may reveal a difference in the culture types perceived by people at different levels or different departments.

Even if you decide not to change your culture type, knowing your type helps you identify risks and weaknesses, so that you can consciously address them. A Community type organisation may need strict rules to prevent corruption. Leaders need to be wary of favouritism come promotion time. A Freelance Agency organisation may need clear rules and penalties regarding salespersons poaching one another's customers. A Young Start-up organisation needs to remind their people to take care of health and family, e.g. offering medical check-up benefits, because they tend to be so absorbed in their work that they forget these.

What Will Work Best for You

After identifying your culture type, how will you know whether it is the right one? If it is not, how do you tell which type you should aim for? In previous sections, we examined the characteristics, strengths and weaknesses of each culture type. The right one for your organisation is one where the strengths help achieve the desired outcomes, and the weaknesses do not severely hinder you. Create multiple scenarios based on real situations in your business, and imagine your organisation behaving in ways reflecting each of the four culture types. This will help you identify which culture type suits you best.

Here are three more angles to help you decide.

Business Fit

The nature of your business determines a large part of your needs. If you tend to have complex projects involving people from different skill backgrounds, the Research University type likely won't work, because you need people to be able to work together. Interestingly, both Community and Freelance Agency types, despite being two different extremes, may work. Community type because a network of close-knit employees can leverage relationships to collaborate well. Freelance Agency type because everyone has a clear understanding of what needs done and how to go about it.

Business fit is not about your industry. Don't be restricted by how your industry typically behaves. Feel free to challenge the norm. If you think a different culture type will work better for your organisation, go for it.

Leadership Fit

Culture change and the change management journey must be driven from the top. Any new culture type you aim for must fit your leadership team, because they must believe in it and help you deploy it. If your leadership team already lives the culture type you want to aim for, you have strong support to proceed to implement the change. If they do not yet practise your targeted culture type, you must make sure this target is compatible with them before you convince them to lead the rest of the organisation in culture change.

People Fit

People fit means looking beyond the leadership team to all members of the organisation. Even if a culture type fits your business needs and your leadership team, you still need to consider whether it will work for the organisation as a whole. If you are running a government department with mostly middle-aged employees near retirement, trying to instil and maintain a Young Start-up culture may not be realistic or beneficial. Considering people fit does not mean sticking to the current culture. If it is right to change, you must be committed to do it. People are naturally resistant to change.

"Changing people is one of the hardest things to do. It is also one of the most valuable things we do."

Changing the culture of an organisation must start from the top. It is the behaviour of leaders, not just what they say, which drives the culture. Actions speak louder than words. Recognising the importance of organisation culture, and being committed to creating the right one for the organisation, are essential to building a high-performing and effective organisation.

Take Action

1. Using the questions in the section *Identifying Your Culture Type*, mark in this table below your YES'. This will help you identify your culture type.

Community	Young Start-up
Research University	Freelance Agency

2. What are the strengths of your current culture type which are beneficial to your business?

3. What are the weaknesses of your current culture type which are hurting or holding back your business?

4. What is your target culture type based on the following three considerations? List the pros and cons.

Business Fit:

Leadership Fit:

People Fit:

Chapter 5: Organisation Evolution

All organisations go through a performance evolution from the day they are formed. Some progress further than others and achieve higher levels of productivity. Sometimes, some divisions, departments or teams evolve further than others. Sometimes, organisations devolve, e.g. due to a change in leadership. Not all organisations reach the highest stage, not even some of the oldest and most established companies in the world. Many settle in the Structured stage.

Understanding the different stages of the organisation evolution allows us to identify where we are, understand the pitfalls and issues, and work towards the next stage(s). You may find that your organisation does not sit squarely within one particular stage; some teams or individuals may demonstrate behaviours of one stage, while others demonstrate behaviours of another stage. Sometimes, the same team or individual may even demonstrate behaviours of different stages. These are common. Your goal is to shift your organisation's behaviours forward to the next stage.

Ad Hoc	Structured	Superstars
• Stuff happens • Survival • No system / structure • Inconsistent leadership • Unclear direction • Unclear responsibility • Reactive • Little communication • Short-term • Act out of fear	• Follow rules • Hierarchy • Command & control • Stability • Belonging, strong group identity • Risk averse • Rigid, efficient • Clear targets • Transactional • Territorial • Blame • Lack trust • Leader knows best	• I'm a star • System supports individual goals • Empowerment • Esteem, pride • Responsible for own performance • Achievement mentality • Values and standards (as opposed to targets) • Delegation

The Ad Hoc Stage

> *Ad hoc – Latin for "to this"; refers to completing a task using an improvised or impromptu method specific for the task, without following any standard structure or process.*

The word commonly used by employees to describe a company in the Ad Hoc stage is "messy". They are not clear about their roles and responsibilities. They are not told the direction of the company. They do not know what the boss wants. They feel instructions and requirements are unclear and keep changing. They do not understand why one piece of work is rejected, while another is praised. People work in a passive and reactive survival mode. I am just trying to get by today. I have no idea what I may be asked to do tomorrow. Employees feel a lack of control. Leaders and managers seem to change their minds too frequently.

Due to uncertainty and operating in a survival mode, employee actions are driven by fear. Fear of making mistakes, fear of being penalised, fear of getting fired. Employees become timid and are reluctant to try new ideas. They do not want to stand out or attract attention. They just want to avoid trouble. They minimise themselves. They are just trying to get through the day in one piece. They don't have long-term aspirations.

Many young organisations find themselves in the Ad Hoc stage, especially when the leadership team is inexperienced. Also, small companies trying to scale up often get into this situation, because they do not yet have strong processes and skills to manage an increasingly complex organisation. Without bringing order to the chaos, an organisation will not scale up well. It needs to evolve to the Structured stage.

One particular company I have worked with had employees telling me that they often had to completely redo a set of graphic designs, and they were told only a few days before the deadline. Project planning was being done, and deadlines were set. Regular meetings were conducted to track progress. There were processes put in place. However, when it came to reviewing and approving work, multiple managers had a say and any single one of them could veto a piece of work, sometimes overturning approvals from other managers. There was no alignment among the approving managers. There was no empowerment to the execution teams to be able to complete their work efficiently. There was no clear single approver for one set of designs. As a result, the execution teams felt directionless, frustrated and demotivated.

The Structured Stage

The Structured stage is all about processes, procedures and clear rules. These are communicated clearly and everyone follows them. Day-to-day operations run smoothly. There is a clear hierarchy in the organisation. Employees are able to work efficiently. They have clear targets to meet. There is a strong sense of belonging. The organisation is stable. All this sounds great, compared to the chaos of the Ad Hoc stage. However, the Structure stage has its limitations and drawbacks too.

A Structured stage organisation is all about command and control. You listen to your boss and you do not question. The boss is always right. Processes are rigid. They are designed to be easy to follow for everyone, i.e. they cater for the lowest common denominator. Don't try to be smart. Don't try to be a hero. Just obey.

Structured stage organisations can be territorial in nature. Every department and team has a clearly defined role and scope. They don't go beyond their boundaries and they expect others not to meddle in their areas. Because of this clear lineation, sometimes a blame culture ensues. When an incident occurs, people are quick to identify whose fault it is, and to distance themselves from the matter if it is not theirs. They are not wrong, just that you end up with a turf mentality.

A Structured stage organisation is not imaginative. It does not think creatively. It is not keen to explore new and better solutions to existing problems. It is resistant to change. It is bogged down by bureaucracy.

One large organisation I have worked with has a very structured culture. They have a comprehensive methodology for managing IT projects. Every project is divided into 6 stages, with specific documentation and deliverables required at every stage, to be reviewed and approved by subject matter experts in specific areas. There are document templates to be followed, review meetings to be conducted and sign-offs to be obtained. These processes help to maintain a certain quality level. There is a standard way of doing things which employees are trained on. Expectations are aligned, which reduces unnecessary rework. These come at a cost. Processes need to be followed and documents prepared, and these take time and effort. The organisation is willing to and can afford to allocate time and effort for them. Projects may not move as fast as other companies' due to all this overhead work, and that is a conscious choice of the organisation.

Inefficiencies can creep in if project managers complete documents for the sake of getting approvals, as opposed to actually utilising these documents based on what they are designed for. For example, test cases need to be developed to properly test a new software to ensure it is bug-free. Employees half-heartedly create test cases, making up the quantity, without actually thinking hard about all the possible situations the end user may encounter. People follow rules but forget the intention behind the rules.

The Superstars Stage

How does an organisation evolve beyond the Structured stage? The answer lies in encouraging and supporting your people to achieve beyond what they believe they are capable of. You want employees who are not content with the status quo, who hunger for more. An organisation which constantly challenges itself is one which will continuously create new value. This is what entrepreneurship and high-performance are about!

In a Superstars stage organisation, ambitious high achievers are well supported by the whole system. They are recognised and rewarded. People take charge of their own success. They hold themselves accountable and they take pride in what they do. To them, achievement is more than just targets to meet. They understand the value in their work. A Superstars type organisation empowers its people so that they can shine. The leaders delegate effectively. The growth mindset permeates the organisation.

The story doesn't end here. Even after evolving to the Superstars stage, there is still room for improvement in the organisation.

The Superstars mentality has its risks and drawbacks. It is primarily about personal gain and individual achievement. You get strong egos and ruthless competition. When you put a dream team of superstars together, sometimes the whole is less than the sum of its parts.

In the 2006 FIBA Basketball World Championship, the USA team of NBA superstars lost to the Greek team, which did not have a single NBA player. The USA dream team included LeBron James, Dwyane Wade and Dwight Howard. Individually, they were dazzling sportsmen and better players, but at this championship they did not come together and leverage one another as well as the Greek team did.

Beyond the Superstars stage, there is one more - the Win Together stage.

Ad Hoc	Structured	Superstars	Win Together
• Stuff happens • Survival • No system / structure • Inconsistent leadership • Unclear direction • Unclear responsibility • Reactive • Little communication • Short-term • Act out of fear	• Follow rules • Hierarchy • Command & control • Stability • Belonging, strong group identity • Risk averse • Rigid, efficient • Clear targets • Transactional • Territorial • Blame • Lack trust • Leader knows best	• I'm a star • System supports individual goals • Empowerment • Esteem, pride • Responsible for own performance • Achievement mentality • Values and standards (as opposed to targets) • Delegation	• We succeed together • Meaning and purpose • Teams that self-govern • Awareness and responsibility to self and others • Care • Collaboration • Honest communication and feedback • Principles • Community spirit

The Win Together Stage

A Win Together stage organisation has a different mindset which makes it seem like a step backwards. Getting to this stage may seem like you are being nice again, and you are going soft. However, you are in fact taking a wiser and more holistic view. You broaden your horizons and see beyond yourself, your team and your organisation. In a Win Together stage organisation, success is not perceived as a zero-sum game. There is more collaboration not only among teammates, but also across teams, departments, divisions and even with external parties. Employees find meaning and purpose and are driven by higher, noble ideals. It is at this evolution stage that members of an organisation do their best work.

Dale Carnegie told a famous story about Andrew Carnegie and George Pullman, two highly successful steel magnates, who were locked in destructive competition. They went after the same customers. They got into a price war. Neither made much profit because of this. A person who is competitive and has a strong ego would double down on his efforts and come up with creative strategies to outdo his opponent. It is just another challenge to overcome, another mountain to climb. However, Carnegie had a different perspective. He met with Pullman and proposed a merger instead. By doing so, they would go on to achieve higher efficiencies, save costs and they both made more money.

At one organisation I led, we once encountered a customer service crisis for a newly launched product. There were many issues with the new product, resulting in many customer complaints and enquiries. There were more new cases per day than the number of cases we could resolve, which meant the total number of cases kept growing. Eventually, customers simply gave up because we could not attend to them in a timely manner. Normally, it was an offshore team which handled such customer interaction. However, due to the volume of enquiries, additional teams were mobilised to help. During this crisis, we had staff members from unrelated teams volunteering to help. They were not customer service experts and there was no reward for taking on extra work. However, they understood and appreciated the importance of resolving this crisis to the whole organisation. They genuinely wanted to help their colleagues. As a result, we managed to bring the number of cases under control swiftly, and we were able to release the temporary helpers earlier than we expected. In a Win Together organisation, people know they can count on one another. Individual success is driven by collective success.

The Culture Evolution Analogy

Here is a simple analogy for the four stages of performance evolution:

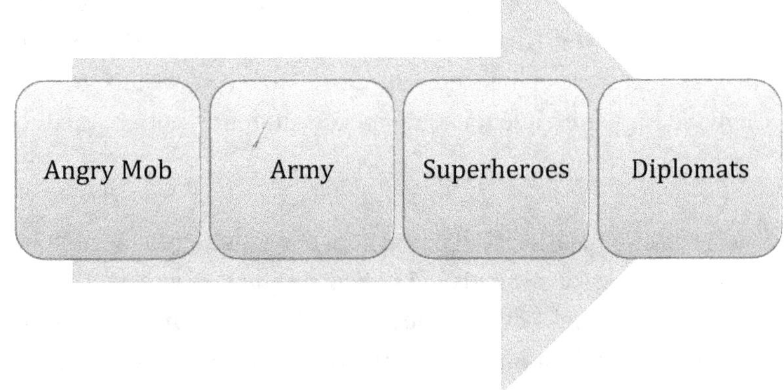

Culture Evolution Analogy

The Angry Mob is disorganised and follows no system. It is reactive and does not have a clear direction. The Army is strict, structured and efficient. However, it is also inflexible and lacks imagination. Superheroes are confident and dazzling. They are competitive and they bring out their best. They aim high and they achieve. The Diplomats believe in mutual benefit and sustainable prosperity. They serve a higher purpose.

Take Action

1. Referring to the summary diagram in this chapter describing the four stages of performance evolution, add a tick to the table below for each description that matches your current organisation. This will give you an idea of where you are at, help you understand why people behave the way they do, and identify what mindsets and behaviours need to be changed.

Ad Hoc	Structured	Superstars	Win Together

2. Break your organisation down into departments, teams or individuals. Do they behave in different ways reflecting different stages of performance evolution? Use the same table to write where each department, team or individual is currently at.

3. For each department or team above, what are the biggest issues that you want to address, or mindsets you want to change?

Part 3: Implementation

Chapter 6: Defining Your Purpose

Why does your organisation exist? What problem do you solve? What value do you bring? Everything the organisation does must reflect its purpose. It is not only important to have a clear purpose, the leadership team must also believe and live this purpose, so that it is cascaded to the rest of the organisation. The purpose must be communicated clearly, consistently and frequently to every member of the organisation, through words and actions.

The "Right" Purpose

Strictly speaking, there is no "right" purpose for an organisation. Depending on what kind of organisation you want to create, and what kind of people you have in your organisation, some purposes can be more "right" than others. At one company I worked with, the CEO proudly declared that his goal was to ring the bell at the stock exchange, i.e. making his start-up company a listed company. Financial success and the prestige of working at a listed company can be the right goals to motivate people. Some people join start-ups precisely because of this; because they believe in the start-up dream, the unicorn start-up. Another CEO I worked with had a very different goal. He wanted to make an online game which was played around the world. That sounded much humbler, but it might be even harder to do given how competitive the industry was. This purpose would resonate with a different type of people.

When you lead an organisation, you should not change the purpose to fit the people. Instead, you should find people who share the same purpose to join you on your mission.

You need to think about not only the purpose, but also how your organisation will fulfil this purpose. What is the strategy, and what do you do every day to achieve your purpose? What makes you different from others who are trying to solve the same problem? What is unique about you? Do you have a clear identity?

Employees are motivated when their personal beliefs are in line with the company's purpose. That is why this purpose must be made clear to everyone. Understanding the purpose is also needed to make everyday decisions. The purpose is your north star. Understanding the objectives of the organisation helps people make the right decisions and work productively. So how do you convey and instil the purpose of the organisation in your people?

Measure What's Important

Measure success and results based on your purpose. All companies report monetary profits on an annual basis because they are established to make money for their shareholders. However, money must not be the only thing you measure. Money is but a proxy for the value the company brings to its customers. You must serve a need or solve a problem, and only when you do that are your customers willing to pay you money. Let's say you are a non-profit organisation. Your most important measure may be the infant mortality rate in your country. Whatever performance is measured on is what people will focus on and try to improve. This is why KPIs (Key Performance Indicators) exist. Whatever you don't measure or report, will likely not get as much attention. Put it on paper in black-and-white, and it becomes what your people will care about.

Relate to Your Purpose

Find every opportunity to show how decision-making is linked to your purpose. When your team needs to consult you on a difficult decision, walk through your thinking process with them, including how you prioritise and how your final decision helps achieve the organisation's goals.

One common situation people encounter is whether to move a deadline. At one of my past projects, where my team developed infographics and copywriting for a client, and were committed to a delivery deadline, we came to a stage where the quality of work was not yet up to par, but time was running out to get things completed. We did not have time to revisit the design concept and redo everything, since we had already communicated the target dates to the client. Any delay was an opportunity cost because the product launch would be delayed, and there would be no profits being generated. There was pressure to go to market. Eventually, the decision-making came back to a mantra I had been telling my team. "We Help People Sell". If we had gone ahead with the content we had at that point, we foresaw poor sales. The purpose would be defeated. So we stuck to our principles, and committed more time to revise and enhance our work, so that it would achieve what we set out to do in the first place. The thought process and rationales were explained to the team and this provided clarity to them not only for this project, but also on how we operated as a company and what our culture and values were.

Praise Desired Behaviours

Praise behaviours which align with the organisation's purpose. People learn from praise. It is a common misconception that people learn from mistakes and thus we should encourage people to make mistakes. We should encourage people to be bold and try new things and we must also help them to succeed. If our people consistently fail and get no support or constructive feedback, they will only become demotivated and give up. Recognise and acknowledge the correct behaviours and your team will display more such behaviours.

I had one team member, let's call him Ian, who was outspoken and sometimes openly challenged company processes or voiced dissatisfactions. Often, such persons are perceived as troublemakers or complainers. They are chastised, especially when they speak up in public, because such behaviour is considered challenging and disrespectful to authority. In Ian's case, I had to address his questions in the public forum, a town hall session for the company where all staff were present. Privately, I spoke to him to reaffirm his positive mindset to raise questions when he saw issues, and to make suggestions when he saw problems. Even if his way of communication was blunt and came across as defiant, the fact that he was proactive in wanting to change for the better must be acknowledged and praised, so that he would continue to hold these values which were important to the company.

Remember to Reflect

Self-reflection is a useful tool. Examine what you do and what your organisation does. Is the work you are doing still relevant to your purpose? Humans are creatures of habit. Often, we get so busy and lost in a rhythm of the same things that we forget to ask ourselves whether the things we spend our time on are still the right things we should be doing.

Many well-known corporations e.g. Dell, Microsoft, IBM, Deloitte, Gap and General Electric have now abolished annual performance appraisals, which have been a standard HR practice especially in large, mature organisations. When such an idea was first suggested, it shocked many HR practitioners. This is an excellent example of reflecting on existing processes and assessing whether they are still relevant. Many companies eventually came to realise how ineffective and costly their performance appraisal processes had been and replaced them with new practices to fit their needs. In some cases, instead of supervisors giving ratings to employees, the performance of employees is measured based on business results.

In many companies, purpose is captured in their vision and mission statements. Unfortunately, sometimes these become something people do for the sake of doing. They become hollow. During orientation, the HR team tells you about them. Three months later, you've already forgotten half of them. We print posters about our vision and mission and stick them up around the office, but if we keep this mentality of doing for the sake of doing, without actually believing and living the purpose, the whole exercise becomes a waste of time.

Define your purpose clearly. Communicate it. Anchor your organisation and your activities around it. With the purpose as your pillar, your people will gravitate towards a value mindset. Whatever fulfils your purpose is of value, everything else is peripheral.

Take Action

1. If you ask the youngest member of your organisation (in terms of who joined you most recently, not age), can he or she clearly articulate the purpose of the organisation? If not, what should be done to better communicate the purpose?

2. How do you currently **measure** success at your organisation? How closely do your KPI's link to your purpose?

3. How often do people **relate** to the organisation purpose when making day-to-day decisions?

4. Are behaviours that align with the organisation's purpose acknowledged and **praised**? Who in the organisation explicitly pays attention to do this? In what form or on which occasions is this done?

5. How often do you and your team **reflect** on your purpose? How do you examine whether your daily activities continue to contribute towards the purpose?

Chapter 7: Building Trust

An organisation, be it a for-profit company, a casual hobby club or a resident association at an apartment block, is made of people. You can't run away from that. When you need a group of people to come together to do something, you need to know how to manage the group of people in order to be able to achieve the objective of the organisation. Having a group of people working together effectively ultimately rests on trust.

Trust takes time to build but can be destroyed in a second. It takes discipline and consistency to build. Building trust depends greatly on the leader and the leadership team of the organisation. Techniques and processes can only get you so far. If the leaders lack integrity and are not truly trustworthy, applying the techniques and processes will only come across as insincere and deceitful. Thus, building trust is all about reflecting on what kind of leader you are and what kind of person you want to be. You do not need to be one specific type of person in order to be a trusted leader. Successful leaders come in many different shapes and sizes. However, you must start with integrity. That is the cornerstone of building trust.

Walk the Talk

This is also known as saying what you mean and meaning what you say. Your actions must be consistent with the ideals you preach to your team. This may sound easy, but the challenge often comes in the form of not even knowing your actions are inconsistent. This is why self-reflection is important. Question decisions you have made. Do not be afraid to admit mistakes and do what is right. Listen to suggestions from your team. These will help as self-checks.

One CEO I worked with, Teck Seng, practiced self-reflection. In most decision-making, he had the final say and he did not always listen to his advisors. However, his team did not shy away from raising objections or offering different opinions. They knew they would be heard and their input would be taken seriously. Sometimes, when Teck Seng's decision led to disaster, he readily admitted it and took responsibility. He went back to the person who had suggested the different solution and told him, "You were right, I should've listened to you."

Be the kind of leader that you would trust. That is one simple way of reflecting on whether you would be a leader that your team trusts. When you pay attention to interactions with your subordinates, it is easy to determine whether they trust you. How they react to what you say, their facial expressions and their body language tell you whether they believe what you say. When you see hesitation and uncertainty, you must put yourself in their shoes, and reflect on whether there is inconsistency between what you say and what you do.

Respect Every Individual

Many leaders have big egos and think of themselves as being above those working for them or holding positions junior to them. One CEO I worked with was well known for making people wait for him. Meetings with him were regularly rescheduled or cancelled. He was always late for meetings. Such behaviour meant he did not respect other people's time. It also reflected poorly on his own time management.

One very simple thing anyone can do to show respect and to build trust is simply being present for the other person. How often have you seen people glance at their phones during meetings? Or texting away on their phones or taking calls? Put that phone away and pay attention to the here and now. There are also people who bring their laptops to meetings and then end up spending most of the time working on their respective tasks unrelated to the meetings. Why not focus, be present, and get the discussion concluded efficiently?

Many business leaders treat employees like pawns. Sometimes, we forget that every employee is an actual person, with his or her own hopes and dreams, values and beliefs. You should treat your employees as partners and companions on the same journey, sharing the same objectives. When we treat people as tools, it is impossible to build trust.

One important skill leaders must have is empathy. A question I often ask job applicants is, "What do you want to get out of this job?" By understanding your employee's goals and motivations, you can better align company and employee objectives. Being able to stand in the other person's shoes is a powerful skill in influencing people. Leadership is all about influencing people.

I have gone as far as encouraging an employee to quit if he is no longer learning, growing, or getting what he wants out of his work. When you truly care for a person, you want what's best for them. If you suppress personal goals for the sake of organisational goals, eventually that person will leave the organisation. A sustainable relationship between individual and organisation must be mutually beneficial.

A previous subordinate, let's call her Veronica, once came to me and said she was offered a position and that the company even offered to sponsor her to further her studies. She wanted my advice. I told her sincerely that she should take the offer. I knew at the time that our company could not offer her something like this. I thought it was an opportunity she should not miss. In the end, she did not take that offer for various reasons. One of the factors was the company culture and team spirit we had. We trusted one another and we took care of one another.

Inappropriate Jokes - one practice many leaders do not take as damaging is inappropriate jokes. This is not limited to mildly sexist, racist or political jokes. One leader I know sometimes jokes to his team that if they didn't deliver results he would cut their salaries. The team understands that he jokes, but to some employees, salaries are a serious matter. They are highly dependent on a stable salary to support their families. The seemingly harmless joke is actually highly uncomfortable. Something which is important to some people, in this case the salary, is taken as the butt of a joke.

Men sometimes joke about young, pretty female job applicants, or which department gets all the good-looking new recruits. There may be no ill intention, but these are best avoided. A leader must demonstrate respect for the individual always and hold his or her leadership team to the same standards.

Practise Fairness

A leader often has to be detached from his or her teams, not because the authority figure needs to be maintained, but because he or she must be an unbiased judge and decision-maker in many situations. Fairness is an important trait to earn and build trust not only in the individual leaders, but also in the system. A good leader must not favour certain employees or groups of employees. In fact, they must not even be *perceived* as being so.

There are some leaders who favour some departments over others. The favoured departments get a bigger say in decision-making. They are entrusted with the bigger projects. Failures are tolerated more, whereas other departments are immediately penalised or blamed. This often results in poor decision-making, fragmentation of the organisation, and eventually, the side-lined and frustrated employees quitting. Some leaders favour staff who have been around for longer, but are particularly unforgiving towards newer staff. Older staff have gained trust and have the advantage of experience in dealing with their work and managing the boss. Because they are in the in group, they enjoy favouritism from the boss. The boss is understanding towards old staff and is more forgiving towards mistakes. New staff are less trusted and are more acutely criticised and scrutinised. Such imbalances break trust in the organisation.

One other aspect of fairness is recognising and rewarding contributions fairly. Bonuses and salary increments should not be a default. They should reflect employee contributions. Employees who do well and contribute must be acknowledged. At the same time, those who did not should not be rewarded. Fairness is meritocracy. Bonuses and increments given to undeserving employees hurt company morale, especially that of hardworking and contributing employees. They undermine any talk of value mindset.

This happened at one company I worked with. One particular project team recorded the highest sales in the previous year and sales of every project was open knowledge at the company.

When it came to declaring annual bonuses for staff, there were debates among the management team on how to award the bonuses. The final decision was that everyone received a flat one-month bonus. The project team that achieved outstanding results were not treated any differently. In the following year, the whole team resigned at various times. The bonuses might not have been the only reason, but it was certainly a contributing factor.

Michael Jordan, one of the best basketball players in NBA history, was well known as a tough leader. He was demanding. He pushed his team hard. However, he never asked them to do something which he didn't do himself. He trained just as hard, or even harder. How many times have we seen bosses who come to the office well past the start of working hours while they expect every employee to never be late for work? They see themselves as above others, above the rules they themselves set. Such behaviour undermines trust. One highly committed team I worked with had a leader who always started work earlier than the rest of his team. He was always ready to jump in to solve a problem when his expertise was needed. This is the type of leader people trust and follow.

Keep Your Word

Keeping your word may not seem hard to do. What is often harder for a busy business leader is to actually remember the promises and commitments you have made. It takes a conscious effort to remember them and to make sure they are carried out. You can delegate, but you must be accountable for the final results.

One young start-up I worked with encouraged its teams by announcing the intention of giving out share options. It was an exciting time. There were opportunities. Employees were hopeful. However, the share options were never seen through. As the company ran into challenges, the matter was simply deprioritised and deferred. There was no follow up and talk of share options just became empty promises from the employees' perspective.

One good example of Keeping Your Word which I have come across, is a company which issued a bonus to employees who had resigned. Typically, once you even decide to leave a company, your bonus would be forfeit, even if your official last day of work was after the bonus issuance date. This particular company believed that the annual bonus was to recognise and reward contributions of employees for the previous financial year. So, even if some employees had resigned, the principle remained true. They wanted to reward the employees for past work which was done well. This practice not only made the ex-employees happy, it also built the trust of current employees.

There are times you need to break a promise. Situations may have changed and made that necessary. In such situations, you have to be transparent about it, and explain why. Going back to the young start-up example, a better approach for handling it was to be open and honest about the challenges the company was facing, and why share options were deferred. Some form of communication would have been better than silence. Alternatively, the start-up could have still gone ahead with the share options, even if share value was not high at the time. One objective of offering share options is to make employees feel like owners and this holds true even when the company is going through a rough period.

Trust Your Team

Trust works both ways. You also need to learn to trust your team. The keyword is empowerment. This is something we often hear, but leaders and managers often have difficulty letting go. We want things done a very specific way. That's the "my way, or the highway" mentality. We end up micromanaging every little decision, wearing ourselves out. The team neither learns nor improves, because they end up always waiting for your precise instructions. They just follow instructions and they don't take accountability of the results. After all, it is your idea, and if it doesn't work, it's not their fault. Hence, the importance of empowerment. You have to let your teams decide and take responsibility for their decisions. That is how they learn. They will make some mistakes, and they will then learn, when they have accountability. This is not to say you are completely hands off and you let them sink. You must still be involved and steer the team if you find the direction completely off course. However, you have to let your teams grow and take ownership.

One of the most powerful forms of encouragement is having high expectations of your team, and making sure they know it. Trevor Moawad told a story about a successful magazine entrepreneur who used to do poorly at school. He was raised by a single mother in the US Midwest. He struggled through school and hung out with the wrong crowd. He promised his mother that he would take the SAT test, and he did. To his surprise, he scored 1480 out of 1600. His mother initially suspected that he cheated, but he did not. He realised that he could do this. He wasn't the failure that everyone, including himself, thought he was. He started attending classes consistently. He graduated and went on to college, eventually going to an Ivy League school. He became a successful entrepreneur.

12 years after that fateful SAT exam, he received a letter from the SAT board. They periodically reviewed their processes, and found that in the year he took the test, 13 students were sent incorrect scores, and he was one of them. His actual score was 740 out of 1600. What this story tells us is when a person has high expectations of himself, he will change his behaviour and mindset, and these changes lead to confidence, productivity and success.

Empowerment is a crucial element in scaling a business. An effective leader must be able to delegate decision-making downwards to every person in the organisation chart. An organisation which is empowered is able to operate efficiently, without needing the leadership team to spoon-feed instructions at every step. Zappos, which sells shoes online, has a famous customer service story. One customer needed to return a pair of shoes, but her mother had just passed away, and she never got around to do it. When the customer service agent found out about it, she arranged for a courier service to pick up the shoes so that the customer didn't need to handle it. She also sent the customer flowers. This customer service agent not only understood the values of the organisation, she was also empowered to take action.

When you trust your team, you build their confidence and competency, and they go on to do amazing things.

Be an Authority Figure

Building trust in your organisation includes building confidence in your leadership capabilities and your competency level. You have to be seen as an expert, being in control, and knowing where the organisation is heading, even though, at times, you may have doubts yourself. There is still a strong leader image you need to portray and maintain. Don't pretend to be someone you are not. Be conscious of what you say and do and how your team sees you. If it isn't helpful, don't do it.

Never tell people how hard you work. You often need to work hard behind-the-scenes to resolve a problem or to learn something new. When you have developed a solution or when you have learned something useful to your team, share them generously and make it seem easy. You don't need to talk about the blood and sweat behind the results you achieved. Showing the results is sufficient. Let them speak for your capability.

When you feel uncertain, be open about it. Discuss with your team and work through it together. Being *vulnerable* and being able to admit what you don't know are signs of confidence. A leader does not need to know everything. A leader needs to be able to fully make use of the knowledge of the team to get things done.

One tricky situation which leaders have to handle is addressing difficult questions at all-staff meetings. This is especially true when you have smart employees who are not afraid to voice their concerns and challenge any inconsistencies they see in the organisation. In such a public forum, the instinct of most leaders is to give a clear and confident answer. That is what we want to do to maintain our authority figure. We are expected to know our stuff. However, if a question does not have a clear answer yet, a better way of addressing it is to say it is being worked on. Admit that there is no solution yet, and commit to give the solution by a certain date. Then by that targeted date, announce that solution. You do not need to show how hard you worked with the relevant teams to find that solution. Just announce the solution. You will have used vulnerability to your advantage, being able to admit it when an issue has arisen and needs to be resolved. You will have asserted your authority by finding the solution for your team.

If you are personally close to your team, beware not to engage in gossip. You can be casual, but you have to stay professional. You must hold yourself to high standards. It is easy to lapse when you are relaxed around your team members. Never forget your role. It may sound depressing or like you can't fully be yourself. It is only a matter of who you want to be, and consciously reminding yourself of that.

Take Action

1. Examine your leadership style and how you carry yourself using the table below.

    a. What behaviours do you notice in yourself which demonstrate to your team each of the principles of building trust? These must be real actions that your team can see you doing.

    b. What are your behaviours which violate the principles of building trust? How will you eliminate them? If there are multiple changes you want to make, list them in order of priority, and start with just the first one. Put a note at your desk to remind yourself.

	Behaviours to Maintain	Behaviours to Change	Priority
Walk the Talk			
Respect Every Individual			
Practise Fairness			
Keep You Word			
Trust Your Team			
Be an Authority Figure			

2. Using the same table, examine your leadership team, based on your perspective of them. You may ask them to perform the same exercise, then compare notes. You may all see things differently.

Chapter 8: Communication - As A Leader

Half of all the problems we encounter in life boil down to poor communications. People miscommunicate, or they are unwilling to communicate, or they fail to communicate effectively. They give up communicating. Many issues remain unresolved because people have given up. Pride and limiting mindsets hold us back from communicating. Sometimes, we are too busy to communicate. We easily give ourselves excuses.

To build a high-performance team which has the value mindset, behaves like entrepreneurs and is constantly learning and growing, you must be able to communicate effectively with your team. You need to shape the team and cultivate the desired mindsets.

Listening

The biggest misconception about effective communication is that communication is about knowing what to say and how to express yourself. The objective of communication is to help your counterpart understand and accept your idea. It is not about making a statement which nobody agrees with or acts upon. An effective listener understands the audience, senses objections and applies his understanding of the audience to overcome the objections. Communication is about reaching mutual understanding; it is not a one-way street. It is only when there is mutual understanding and empathy on both sides that a common ground can be found.

People with a tendency to dominate a conversation often say, "...you know what I mean?" They are impatient in getting their points across. They have much to say, and they don't listen. If you catch yourself doing this often, pause, and give your counterpart a say. Ask open questions. Ask for their opinion. Don't judge.

Communication fails when people listen in order to answer, not to understand. Before your counterpart finishes the sentence, you are already constructing a counter argument. It is important to see and appreciate more perspectives, before constructing a precise and balanced proposal.

Don't interrupt. It is rude and shows lack of respect. If you are interrupted inappropriately, politely ask, "can you let me finish my point?"

It is better to speak less, and make every statement well thought out and fair. When you demonstrate that you understand your counterpart's perspective, you earn trust and communication becomes much easier. When people feel heard, they are more willing to hear your perspective in return. They don't need to keep trying to make their point if they see that you have taken the point.

Psychological Safety

Psychological safety is championed by Google as the key element to build effective teams. Google employs geniuses. People work hard and are expected to be exceptional in their fields. Everyone knows that everyone else is smart and because of that, they are afraid to show any sign of weakness. They need to be as good as everyone expects them to be. They feel they have to constantly prove themselves. A study done showed that because of this, some teams performed below expectation. The missing key was psychological safety. One particular leader at Google, Matt Sakaguchi, had a team with this problem. At a session discussing his team's survey results, he asked his teammates to share something personal about themselves. He himself started off by telling everyone he had Stage 4 cancer and had been living with cancer for the past 5 years. It shocked the team, which had been working with him for some time and did not know this. At this session, his teammates gradually opened up, and they got to know one another much better. This was the pivotal point where they created psychological safety.

Having psychological safety is when people do not need to constantly keep their guard up. People are willing to communicate, to voice their opinions, to propose different ideas, without fear of being belittled or penalised. Many leaders claim that they are open to suggestion but in practice, they are dismissive towards most of the proposals presented to them. This is a case of actions not matching words – not Walking the Talk. When a leader behaves this way, his team soon stops volunteering ideas. There is no psychological safety and they feel voicing up is futile. Without psychological safety, people feel judged all the time. For a leader to create psychological safety, it is not as simple as making a statement that suggestions are welcome. It is even more important to listen and to take suggestions offered seriously.

Vulnerability is a strength. When a leader dares to be vulnerable, like Sakaguchi was, it shows confidence and it also shows that you are human. People relate to you. They trust you. They feel safe.

Purposeful Repetition

Important messages need to be communicated again and again. Changing an organisation's culture is not about one memo from the Managing Director, one town hall meeting or one full-day leadership workshop. It needs to be done *regularly* and *consistently*. It needs to be done through both words and actions. Instilling mindsets and value systems is done through cultivating habits. When the value mindset and the learning mentality are applied over and over through daily work, they become second nature.

At global oil and gas company, Shell, all meetings start with the host explaining emergency procedures in case of fire or natural disasters - where the emergency exits are, where the assembly point is and any other safety measures to take note of. A new employee may find this awkward, but soon, it becomes natural and a culture of emphasising occupational safety is built through repetition and discipline.

The Wesley Methodist School Principal signs off every memo to staff or parents with the school motto - "Above and Beyond". As a parent, I can't forget the motto even if I wanted to. I am reminded of it all the time. Messages which are important enough warrant repetition, even if it gets tiresome or people make fun of the repetition. When it comes to decision-making time, people will remember the key principles which have been drilled into them consistently.

Say It 5 Times

Busy leaders sometimes tell their subordinates, "Write this down and don't make me repeat myself," or "I'm not going to say this a second time." Some Japanese corporations do the exact opposite. They apply a method called Say It Five Times. This is how it works:

"Maeda-san, please do this task by completing A, B and C. " ......①

"Yes sir, on it!"

"Wait, before you go, Maeda-san, please explain to me in your own words what it is that you will be doing." ......②

"Okay sir. You asked me to perform this task, and I am to follow steps A, B and C. I'll get it done and report back to you before the end of the day. "

"Excellent. Before you go, do you understand the purpose of completing this task? " ......③

"Yes sir. My understanding is that by completing this task, we will be able to achieve objective D. Is my understanding correct sir?"

"Well done, Maeda-san. "

"Thank you. I'll get going sir. "

"Wait, wait. Just a moment. Before you go, can you let me know, based on your experience, what the possible issues are, and how you would manage them? " ......④

"Well, sir, it is possible that we may run into situations E, F and G. If E or F happens, I will do this and this. If G happens I will come back and consult you. Will this be alright sir? "

"Very good! I fully agree with your assessment. One last thing, Maeda-san. If you were to do this task yourself, would you do it any differently? Is there any better way that you would suggest? " ......⑤

"Now that you mention it sir, I'd like to suggest that instead of C, we can do H, which would cost less but achieve the same results. Shall I proceed as such? "

"Good thinking, Maeda-san. Let's do it this way."

In this conversation, the manager went through 5 steps to ensure his team member fully understood what was required and was able to handle the task and achieve the objective. Clear, upfront communication reduces unnecessary rework.

1. The first step was a simple statement of the task.
2. The second step required the executor to repeat what was said in his own words, thus confirming his understanding.
3. The third step of checking whether the executor understood the objective behind the task made sure that his understanding was not just at the surface level. He must understand the underlying reason.
4. The fourth step explored the contingencies. The executor went through the thought process of considering the "what ifs." He knew what incidents he was authorised to make decisions on, and what needed to be escalated for direction. This was built upon his understanding of the underlying purpose of the task.
5. Finally, the executor was given freedom to think of his own solutions. This encouraged him to take ownership and to come up with his own ideas, which might work even better than the original instructions.

The 5-step process may sound excessive, but compared to having your team spend one week doing the wrong thing and then having to redo from scratch, this practice is a sound investment of your time and effort.

Explain Both Good and Bad

Giving feedback is not enough. A good leader must give feedback not only on improvements needed, but also on positive behaviour. Positive behaviour must be reinforced, and negative behaviour avoided. In both positive and negative feedback, the reasoning must be explained. It is in explaining that the values and the mindsets of the organisation are conveyed.

When an employee makes the wrong decision, don't stop at instructing him or her on what to do instead. You must also explain why. When an employee completes an outstanding piece of work, you must not only recognise it, but also specify what he or she did right, and why it was the right thing to do. Don't stop at shallow remarks. Highlight the exact qualities which make a deliverable good or bad.

Praising a user interface design as "nicely done" is not very helpful. Instead, point out how the Call To Action button is being emphasised and is repeated throughout the webpage, how the use of a person's face directs the eyeball of the viewer to the product, or how a partially shown image entices the viewer to scroll down further to see the full image.

Good leaders are able to see the good in the bad, and recognise both. Picture this scenario. An angry customer brings in a defective product and demands a refund. She doesn't want a replacement because she has lost confidence in the product. To appease the customer and to retain her, the salesperson serving her recommends a similar product of a different brand and offers to replace the defective product with it. The customer accepts and leaves happily with the new product. The salesperson has violated company policy. That must be made clear to him. He needs to be trained on the correct procedure to follow. However, the fact that he has solved a customer's problem and created a satisfied customer must also be recognised. It is a behaviour and a mindset to be reinforced.

Take Action

1. Using the table below, reflect on incidents in the past 2 weeks where you have exercised one or more of the best practices.

2. Also based on the past 2 weeks, identify opportunities where you could have exercised one or more of these best practices. This will help you become more alert of such opportunities in future. You may also proactively plan to apply the best practices.

	Occurrences	Opportunities	How To
Listening			Self-awareness
Psychological Safety			Examine habits and change them
Purposeful Repetition			Deliberate planning
Explaining Why - Good and Bad			Self-awareness

3. Using the same table, reflect on both occurrences and opportunities in your leadership team.

4. This is a handy cheat sheet to help you practise Saying It 5 Times. Put it on your phone, on your computer desktop, or at your desk.

THE SAY-IT-5-TIMES TECHNIQUE		
I	I Tell You	This is what I need you to do
Y	You Tell Me	Explain in your own words what you need to do
O	Objective	What are we trying to achieve by doing this?
S	Scenarios	What can go wrong? What would you do?
A	Alternatives	Is there a better way to do this?

Chapter 9: Communication - As an Organisation

An organisation communicates to its members through processes and rules. They embody the values and priorities of the organisation. How you operate an organisation, and what you choose to do on a daily basis, communicates a lot to the members of the organisation.

Transparent Targets and Results

At one organisation I led, we struggled with flagging sales. To better focus and motivate my teams, I introduced a new practice. I created one spreadsheet which was visible to every person in the organisation. The monthly sales targets of every project team were publicised. The actual sales were updated into the spreadsheet every week and a simple projection was done to see whether based on current results, the project would achieve its monthly target by the end of the month. We had quarterly targets to achieve and a projection was done on that too, so that everyone was clear whether we were on track to hit our target, or if we were ahead or behind. We started off being way behind, and it looked hopeless. The first month's results were disastrous. However, it was mostly due to the momentum of past months. When we started this very transparent way of tracking and announcing progress and results, everyone took accountability and took aggressive steps to improve sales of their respective projects. There were clear goals and people knew what to aim for. They came up with concrete and practical actions which would help achieve those goals.

By the end of the first quarter, we had turned things around, caught up, and met our quarterly target. We went on to not only hit but exceed our quarterly targets. Three quarters later, we increased our sales by 90%.

This is how powerful transparency and accountability can be.

Google applies similar principles in their OKR practice - Objectives and Key Results. Every person in the organisation, no matter how junior or senior, has an OKR which is regularly reviewed and assessed. The Objective describes what is to be achieved, and the Key Results are measurable parameters. Being measurable is important because there will be no ambiguity on whether they are achieved or not. Other organisations which use OKR include Spotify, LinkedIn, Twitter, ING Bank, Target and The Guardian.

Regular Meetings

The number 1 thing about the workplace that people love to hate is meetings. The first thing people think of when it comes to meetings is they are a waste of time. "I'd rather be back at my desk doing real work." People hate meetings because many people do not use or conduct meetings effectively. Indeed, many meetings can be replaced with a phone call, an email, or a 5-minute chat in the corridor. The first thing I will say about meetings is don't have them if they are not useful.

Regular meetings are a necessity. The keyword being "regular". Meetings are all about communication. To build a common mindset, rapport and a strong culture requires good communication and interaction among your people. Being regular means people can prepare for it and make the most of it. It means there is no surprise and people plan their schedules around it. They are not disruptive, unlike ad hoc meetings. Regular meetings also give us *discipline* to constantly reflect and review. They build a tempo for how the team operates, and help the team be efficient. They are your constant follow-up to make sure things are moving and things get done.

Albert Einstein once said about physics, "Everything should be made as simple as possible, but no simpler." This applies to meetings too. Meetings should be as short as possible, but no shorter. Unnecessarily long meetings waste time. Meetings forcibly cut short defeat the purpose if the objectives are not achieved. Every meeting must have:

1. A clear objective - To be stated up front by the chairperson.
2. An agenda - Prepared beforehand and communicated to attendees. When appropriate, materials to be distributed beforehand and attendees are to read them before the meeting, as opposed to having presenters go through long and detailed explanations.
3. Action items - Documented during the meeting then communicated to all attendees. Action items must have target dates and must be followed up to completion.

The frequency of meetings depends on the needs of the team and the purpose of the meeting. Working level teams may do weekly meetings due to the need to keep close tabs. Some smaller teams do daily huddles or scrum meetings to quickly align. They move fast and adjust quickly. A more senior level meeting to review company profit and loss may only be done monthly, so that there is enough new information for meaningful discussion and strategising. Frequency must be fit-for-purpose.

Town Halls

Some organisations call them staff meetings or all-hands briefings. Town hall meetings are where all members of an organisation are involved. The nature is more of cascading information and less of interactive discussions, although a Q&A session is usually important. The purpose of town hall meetings is to communicate the status, strategy and direction of the organisation. They bring together the whole organisation, and remind all members about the core values and purpose of the organisation. Communication at town hall meetings is direct from the top. This is when even every junior recruit will feel connected to the CEO. If you want your junior executive to think like a boss, he or she needs to see, hear and learn from the boss.

Town hall meetings let everyone in the organisation know what is going on in other parts of the organisation. When an employee has the grand strategic view of her company, she will make better decisions because she understands the implications of her decision. She may be interested in a new project and volunteer to get herself involved. She will be able to identify more opportunities for collaboration when she has good awareness of what other teams in the company do, what they are good at and what challenges they are facing.

Town hall meetings are used to address any concern staff may have. E.g. when there is political unrest in some countries where a multinational corporation operates, clear guidelines and policies regarding how business is to be conducted, what employees are required to do and whether traveling will be restricted all need to be communicated. The leadership team must also explain the rationales and principles behind the decisions. Many times, town hall meetings are for such practical needs for communicating policies and actions required. Yet through such communication, members of the organisation are reminded of its core values and its position on a subject matter. The values and the purpose of the organisation are reemphasised.

When you treat every employee as a stakeholder of your company, and share updates with them like they are shareholders, they will feel ownership and a sense of belonging towards the company, and they will think more like you. An employee who does not understand what his company is doing, and why, will only have a narrow view - he just wants to complete his tasks and collect his salary.

Surveys

Employee satisfaction surveys are one way to get a pulse on your people. A survey is a two-way communication. It is not just about the company collecting information from its employees. The fact that a survey is being done communicates to people that the organisation respects every individual and seeks feedback. It is important that survey results, good or bad, are summarised and shared with everyone. Concrete actions must be taken on key issues identified. The outcomes of these actions must also be announced. Surveys are not done for the sake of making the management look good. They are for the good of the whole organisation.

Subsequent surveys should compare results against previous surveys, to recognise what has improved, and to identify what has worsened and needs attention. Regular surveys (e.g. every half year) apply the same concept as regular meetings - have the discipline to make sure concrete actions are done.

Ideally, surveys are anonymous, so that there is no fear of retaliation. People feel safe to speak up. A survey should not identify a person. In some surveys, an employee is required to state his team, but if there are only 3 or 4 members in his team, it may be easy for his supervisor to guess that a certain negative comment came from him. The survey must be designed carefully to consider such situations.

Surveys are strong communication tools because they can trigger actions and these actions lead to real outcomes which all affected parties can see.

Surveys are not limited to employees. They apply to customers too. Being a learning organisation means constantly learning from customers too. Customers have no obligation to fill in surveys. Sometimes, it is angry customers who are most keen to do so to give you a piece of their minds. It is important not to take feedback at face value. It is important to think beyond that and seek deeper insights to get to the root cause of a problem.

One story tells of a hotel manager who received many complaints about lifts at the hotel being too slow. She initially looked into upgrading the lifts, but the costs were prohibitive. She studied the waiting times and was surprised to find that they were not long at all. The problem was not with the lifts being too slow. It was with guests feeling bored while waiting for the lifts. Eventually, the solution was to install mirrors at the lift lobby. That gave guests something to do while waiting. They could examine themselves, adjust their hair or clothing, or look at other guests without appearing to be staring.

Enticing customers to complete surveys can be done in many ways, e.g. appealing to a nobler cause, picking the right moment when the customer feels gratified, or offering a gift or discount. Preferably, make the surveys short, so that customers don't give up halfway.

Performance Appraisals

The fact that many large professional corporations abolished performance appraisals made the news. In truth, it was not that they were abolished, but that they were transformed. The old rigid way was no longer effective. Performance appraisals need to be more instantaneous. They should no longer be a long, convoluted annual process which ultimately fails to achieve what it is meant to. Performance appraisals are about communicating with your people. They need to be done regularly and in small doses. They don't need to be very formal. The purpose is to give feedback to your people, to coach them, and to help them improve. It should not be something reviewed only once a year.

Strong communication between employee and supervisor must be established at all levels of a company. It is through these relationships that the purpose and values of an organisation are cascaded to all members. It is how trust is established. Performance appraisals should focus on developing people and that is an ongoing activity tied to tasks, deliverables and projects. People grow through what they do every day and what is communicated every day.

Making performance appraisals a daily habit requires a change in mindset. We need to review how we interact with our subordinates and peers on a daily basis. One way is to consciously set aside time for self-reflection each week - to examine whether there is any positive or negative feedback that needs to be communicated but has not been given. Another way is to schedule weekly or fortnightly one-on-one sessions with direct reports. This helps instil discipline in ourselves.

Team Building Activities

The purpose of team building activities is simple. It is to build stronger communication and ties through activities outside of day-to-day work. When an organisation grows, it becomes harder for everyone to know everyone else. Separate small and informal groups will form, through personal preferences of the employees. Employees only get to know the people they need to deal with in their work.

Some people see team building activities as a chore and a superficial exercise which takes them away from real work. Certainly, I have encountered business leaders and managers who (a) do not show up, or (b) think of team building activities as something for the team leaders to run and the team members to have fun with. When the leader is not participative, that sends a message to the organisation. On the other hand, I have also witnessed leaders who play actively in sports events and who get dumped into the swimming pool together with juniors. These leaders communicate a different message.

A Win Together type organisation requires a collaborative mindset and collaboration requires network building. Team building activities create new connections and networks among members of an organisation, often through a context unrelated to work. Why does a software development company arrange for its staff to go white water rafting as a team building event? It is completely unrelated to the industry. The reason is, the objective is to create and strengthen bonds, not to train staff in rafting.

Team building is not just a feel-good exercise. It shapes the organisational culture and creates synergy.

Terminations

Terminations are unpleasant but necessary. When an employee's personal goals contradict the company goals, or when his or her core values diverge significantly from the team's beliefs, it is better to let him or her go. Sometimes, they resign by themselves. Sometimes, as the leader of an organisation, you have to make that tough call to terminate an employee who is not a fit for the organisation.

Terminations and resignations must be handled with respect, dignity and integrity. It is not only about treating the departing employee with respect, it is also about adhering to core values and principles of the organisation, and instilling the right team culture.

Do not avoid the difficult conversation with the employee who is leaving. Be open and honest. Exit interviews must be done when possible. Often, it is when people are leaving and have nothing to lose that they are willing to speak their minds. This is valuable input and a source of learning. Even if you disagree with what is said, listen and reflect whether comments from the departing employee hint at unspoken issues in the organisation.

Never threaten employees with termination. An employee living in fear is unproductive, uncreative, and only plays safe. Fear spreads and is toxic to team morale. Communicate with and give feedback to underperforming employees, with the intention of helping them succeed by giving them the necessary support and resources. When your employees have the value mindset and understand that everyone must contribute value, they will understand your termination decisions.

Take Action

1. Examine existing processes at your organisation. Which aspects are running well and helping you build the culture you want? Which aspects will you improve?

	Running Well	**To Improve**
Transparent Targets & Results		
Regular Meetings		
Town Halls		
Surveys		
Performance Appraisals		
Team Building Activities		
Terminations		

2. For each aspect to improve, what is the next action required, by whom, and when (date)?

Culture Implementation Framework

Chapters 6 to 9 can be summarised in this diagram below. They form the framework of how you can drive culture transformation at your organisation. You start with the core, and then build upon it. Each outer layer relies on the previous layer to be firm, without which it cannot be developed or deployed effectively.

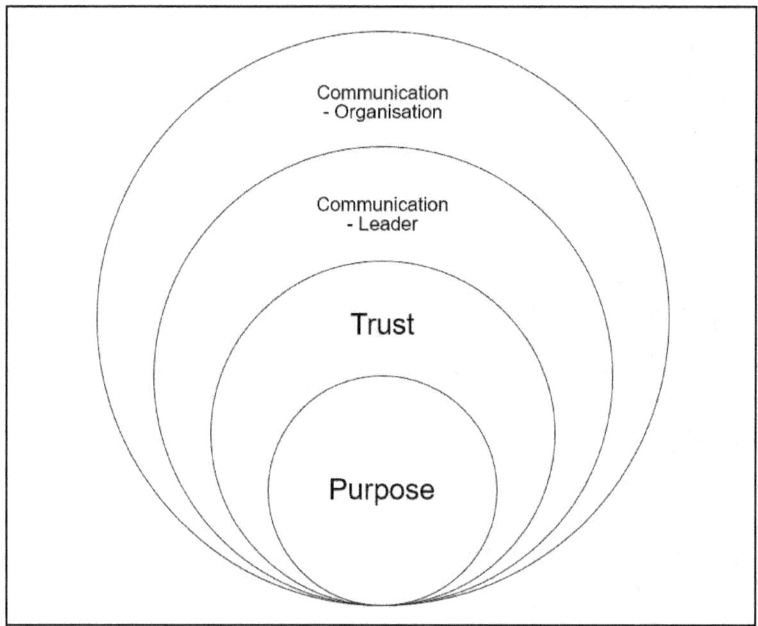

Culture Implementation Framework

At the very core, you start with the purpose of your organisation. It is the goal that all members of the organisation must align to. The next foundation is trust, which must be built and maintained for the rest of the processes and best practices to be built upon.

The next layer – Communication as a Leader – is about personal qualities and how you carry yourself. Gerald Weinberg said, "If you cannot manage yourself, you have no business managing others." This layer is primarily about how the leader and leadership team in an organisation should behave, but the lessons are useful to all members of the organisation. Finally, the layer Communication as an Organisation are the operational practices which shape and sustain the culture of an organisation.

This framework is also a tool to help you diagnose issues with your organisation culture. As you examine layer by layer, you can find the root causes of issues, and sometimes they are buried deeper than you expect.

Chapter 10: OTJM

One simple and useful tool which reflects the value mindset is the OTJM:

1. Objective
2. Target Audience
3. Job to Be Done
4. Metrics

This tool can be applied to all tasks, big or small, and helps to remind people of the value perspective. When taking on a new task, a new job assignment or even a large project, defining the OTJM upfront ensures that the direction is clear, and you do not waver or get distracted.

Objective

Sounds simple? Yet very often, people perform tasks assigned to them without understanding (or caring) about the objective. Sometimes, the objective was never communicated properly to them. Any task, big or small, must have an objective. If the objective is not clear, it must be clarified. If the objective is invalid, don't waste time working on the task. When you play a Child role in the learning model, you ask why. You challenge assumptions. The first step of doing a task is verifying and understanding the objective.

A clearly defined objective makes sure you stay on the path and not waste effort on activities that do not help toward the objective. This is a practical application of the value mindset. Know what is of value and what is not.

I will illustrate the application of OTJM using Mahjong 3P, a top mobile game app on Google Play Store and Apple App Store which I have worked on before. Being a freemium game, it was free-to-play, but players could purchase in-game items which would make the game more enjoyable for them. At the time, despite being a niche game in a niche market, we had tens of thousands of players. 99% of our players were non-spenders, which was typical of the mobile game industry. Our revenue came from only 1% of players who were spenders. We did not display advertisements in our game, and we decided to do this. We wanted to monetise that 99% of our players who were non-spenders. They cost us money, in terms of servers we needed to maintain, customer service we had to provide and in-game events we organised. Why not monetise them? So our objective was to make money off these non-spending players. We would earn money for every advertisement shown to them.

Target Audience

Usually, when you undertake a task, there is a target audience whom you want to change the behaviour of, or that task is meant to serve. For example, Airbnb targets young adults who enjoy traveling, who have small budgets, but do not mind simple or shared accommodation. A political campaign run via social media may target young urban voters who are most concerned about the economy and job stability. Having clarity on your target audience allows you to focus and customise your strategy. You know what makes them tick. You get straight to their pain point.

Returning to the Mahjong 3P example, the target audience was simply the non-spenders. Most of them were not very competitive. They played casually and did not actively participate in in-game contests. Some of them who did play a lot always looked for ways to gain gems (the in-game currency) efficiently without needing to spend real money. They didn't mind spending time and effort to earn just a few gems. Minor inconveniences weren't a big issue, as long as they could play and the game was fun to them. By understanding the target audience, a solution can be developed and customised to fit the purpose.

Job to Be Done

The job to be done refers to the need of the target audience you fulfil. What problem do you solve? What's in it for them? Why would they do what you want them to do? What motivates them? Why is your product so good that they would be willing to spend that kind of money on it? The value mindset perspective must be applied in both directions. You have an objective to fulfil. That is what's valuable to you. You must look at what the objective of your target audience is. If you want them to behave in a certain way, e.g. voting for you, you must create a reason or motivation to drive that behaviour.

Mahjong 3P was a freemium game, so players could download and play it for free. The non-spenders were unwilling to spend money, and they were content with enjoying fewer features in the game. The advertisements we were going to show were interstitial advertisements, which meant these players were forced to watch them after they finished playing a match. This was unlike incentivised advertisements where players were given small rewards for watching ads. In this case, the job to be done was simply being able to continue to play the game. If a player was unwilling to watch any ads, he would have to stop playing the game. We understood that non-spenders were happy to tolerate minor inconveniences in order to continue playing the game for free. Thus, the interstitial ads model would work. It was a willing trade.

Metrics

Defining the metrics for success means agreeing on what constitutes success. Success must be measurable and unambiguous. Metrics are important because by measuring we learn, and by learning we improve. By defining a measurable goal upfront, we set up a benchmark to work towards. Regardless of success or failure, we will learn. If the task is completed successfully, we learn what works. It can mean if we end up doing something similar in future, we should apply the same techniques. It can also mean we have discovered a new opportunity, and we can further explore and experiment, building on top of the initial success to further grow.

If we fail at the task, we learn too. We learn what doesn't work, and we may decide to try again, taking a different approach. "Fail fast, learn fast" is the mantra of lean start-ups. We may realise that the whole exercise has been based on completely wrong assumptions, and decide to abandon the project and cut our losses.

The purpose of having metrics is to learn, and thus be able to make better decisions moving forward.

Returning to the Mahjong 3P example, our metrics were simple - we wanted to earn X amount per month once we started having ads. We also wanted to make sure we did not severely harm our player experience. Thus, we had secondary metrics of matches played per day and Daily Active Users. By measuring these, and tracking them as we made adjustments to our design, we were able to fine tune how we implemented ads in our game.

Case Study - Applying OTJM

At one stage of implementing ads, we had a design which looked like this:

Spender Category	Advertisement Frequency
Non-spender	Every 10 minutes
Low spender (below USD 10)	Every 20 minutes
High spender (above USD 10)	Every 30 minutes

We had a timer in the app which tracked how long a player had been playing. Once the time limit which corresponded with the spender category was reached, the app prepared to display an ad the next time the player completed a match. We did not display an ad halfway through a match because that would disrupt the player experience. This design above was logical. It made sense to show fewer ads to spenders, especially the high spenders.

However, when we revisited our OTJM, one problem became evident. Our target audience was non-spenders. Why would we want to show ads to our spenders at all? The non-spenders already covered 99% of our players. Covering that 1% of spenders would generate little ad revenue, and run the risk of upsetting the spenders. Spenders were typically players who were willing to spend money to save time and remove inconveniences. Why would we want to annoy them and distract them from playing and spending? Our design was quickly rectified:

Spender Category	Advertisement Frequency
Non-spender	Every 10 minutes
~~Low spender (below USD 10)~~	~~Every 20 minutes~~
~~High spender (above USD 10)~~	~~Every 30 minutes~~

Revisiting our OTJM also allowed us to think of a new way to entice non-spenders to become spenders. Once ads were introduced, we created a banner in the game saying, "Spend USD5 and remove ads FOREVER". This was an attractive offer and helped to create new spenders. In mobile games, this was important because the first purchase was the most crucial in changing a player's mindset to believe that it was worthwhile to spend money on a free-to-play game. Thereafter, the player would be more likely to continue to spend.

The OTJM method encapsulates the value mindset and the learning attitude. It is simple to apply and yields great benefits.

Take Action

1. Practice filling the table below for each of the scenarios below:
   a. A task you are working on which takes less than 4 hours
   b. A task you have assigned to another person which takes between 3 to 5 days
   c. A team project you are part of which takes between 2 to 9 months

O	Objective	
T	Target Audience	
J	Job to Be Done	
M	Metrics	

2. For items 1(b) and 1(c), ask the other persons involved to fill in the OTJM table. Check that your understanding is aligned. If it is not, how will you address the gaps?

Chapter 11: Breaking Rules

Having covered many techniques and processes that can be applied to create an entrepreneurial culture, I will now tell you that sometimes, you need to forget all that. The last thing the entrepreneurial spirit needs is being bound by rules and procedures. Facebook's motto, "move fast and break things", may not be as popular as it used to be, but it still captures much of the entrepreneurial spirit. It is adventurous and daring. It challenges convention. It is not afraid to try and fail, then learn and improve.

All rules and processes that have been implemented need to be re-evaluated. We always return to the value mindset. Processes are meant to help you. If they no longer help you, or if they are just creating more work for you without giving enough value, discard them or change them. Your time is precious. Spend it on something of value. That is why sometimes, you need to break your own rules.

It is important to keep in mind the principles - the value mindset, thinking like a boss, and the learning attitude. These are the behaviours of entrepreneurs you want to instil in your people. All rules and processes being implemented must support these, and should only be maintained if they continue to be relevant.

Endnotes

Robert Kiyosaki said that the 3 main management skills needed for success are management of cash flow, systems and people. Many companies have the right business model and the right product, but fail to grow or even survive, because their leaders fail to build a culture for success. They are poor at people management, or they simply deprioritise or neglect it.

Creating an entrepreneurial culture starts with the leadership team of an organisation. By anchoring the organisation to the three Success Factors as guiding principles, they can chart a course toward building the kind of organisation they want, which will best serve their business, and bring out the best in their teams.

Further Reading

1. *The 21 Irrefutable Rules of Leadership* by John C Maxwell
2. *The Lean Startup* by Eric Ries
3. *What Holds the Modern Company Together?* by Rob Goffee & Gareth Jones, Nov-Dec 1996 issue of Harvard Business Review.
4. *The Performance Management Revolution* by Peter Cappelli & Anna Tavis, Oct 2016 issue of Harvard Business Review.
5. *Coaching for Performance* by Sir John Whitmore
6. *Replicable Leadership* by Fan Deng (book is in Chinese, 《可复制的领导力》- 樊登)
7. *Trillion Dollar Coach* by Eric Schmidt, Jonathan Rosenberg, Alan Eagle
8. *How to Win Friends and Influence People* by Dale Carnegie
9. *The Rules of Work* by Richard Templar
10. *The Rules of Management* by Richard Templar
11. *Rich Dad Poor Dad* by Robert Kiyosaki
12. *The Insider's Guide to Culture Change* by Siobhan McHale
13. *Harvard Business Review*, Harvard Business School Publishing Corporation

About the Author

Hiew Chok Sien helps his clients develop high-performance organisation cultures. He coaches leadership teams and helps them transform their organisations to achieve higher effectiveness and to support further growth of their organisations.

Chok Sien has served at multinational companies and young start-ups across different company cultures. Corporations he has served in include Accenture, Standard Chartered Bank, SEGA and Shell. He has worked in diverse industries, from financial services and oil & gas to consulting, mobile games and e-commerce. He started his career in Information Technology, being an honours graduate in Computer Science from Monash University, Melbourne. Throughout his career, he has driven multiple nationwide and regional deployment projects, changing people, process and technology. His work has brought him to Taiwan, Hong Kong, the Philippines, Pakistan, Korea, the USA and Spain. Roles he has served in include Operations Director, Country Manager and Chief Operations Officer.

Chok Sien founded Simplify People, with a mission to help organisations achieve high-performance through developing their leaders and instilling the right organisation cultures.

Chok Sien is a certified professional trainer and business coach. He is currently based in Kuala Lumpur, Malaysia.

Chok Sien can be contacted at cs@simplifypeople.com.